YOUR PLACE
or mine?

GARY MEHIGAN + George Calombaris

Photography by Mark Chew + Simon Griffiths

Illustrations by Andrew Joyner

LANTERN
an imprint of
PENGUIN BOOKS

Foreword

I first met George and Gary some years ago at the Melbourne Food and Wine Festival, where we were each hosting master classes and book signings. Their enthusiasm was infectious and I thoroughly enjoyed watching them strut their stuff. I subsequently led a team of contestants on *MasterChef Australia*, where George and Gary continue their professional collaboration, guiding, educating and challenging the contestants to reach a level beyond amateurs.

They are both chefs with successful restaurants. They know how to judge and execute fine food, and push boundaries without being wild or gimmicky. This cookbook is full of yummy flavours, with dishes suitable for every day as well as special moments. George and Gary love and respect their ingredients, so therefore keep them pure and uncluttered. This is cooking as it should be — taking the best ingredients, then treating them with care and relishing the results.

This book will no doubt fly off the shelves.

Happy eating and good cooking.

Michel Roux

Chef Patron, The Waterside Inn, Bray

Contents

BUTCHER

FISHMONGER

Chef to Chef

GARY ON GEORGE

I employed George Calombaris in an apprentice intake at the Hotel Sofitel in Melbourne in the mid-1990s. He was seventeen and fresh-faced, with loads of hair. George stood out from his peers. He was a hard worker, passionate and driven, but he was also nervous as anything – he used to get the jitters, which was something to do with his blood sugar, I think. The apprentices were exposed to every area of the hotel kitchen, from pot washing to pastry, butchery and fine dining. It was similar to the classical training that I had had at the Connaught in London, where you learned perfection through repetition.

When I left Sofitel to open Fenix with Raymond Capaldi, management was worried that I'd strip the kitchen of staff. But I only took two chefs; one was George. He was hungry for success, and so he jumped at the opportunity. I think he learned creativity from Raymond and management from me. He learned how to run a business from the mistakes we were making. Over time our relationship changed; he was no longer George the apprentice but rather an integral part of our success. We kept promoting him until he was head chef. Fenix was, and still is, a busy place and service could be brutal. We'd go through a hell of a service, George and I would look at each other amid the fury of the hot stoves, the orders and the stress – and we'd just keep it together.

You get to know someone very well when you're standing next to them for twelve hours a day. I like to think I've been a mentor to George, and played some part in shaping who he is today. He left Fenix to work at Reserve, which was not the most successful venture – it went under – and, as a friend, I was really concerned about him. Later at The Press Club I was pleased to see George reach a turning point where he realised that regardless of how amazing and avant garde his food was, there was something more to success than being flash. It's been a great pleasure for me to see him embracing his background and reinventing Greek food.

Our paths crossed frequently, even when we didn't work together. My wife, Mandy, and I went to his wedding, and to his house for dinner. I was there for him when he got divorced.

As part of an ambitious chef's portfolio, doing a bit of media work is the way to go, and we both did a bit of that. And then the opportunity to audition for *MasterChef Australia* came up. When I was shortlisted I called George and found out that he'd been shortlisted too, and we travelled to Sydney to audition together. I noticed all these big egos – all well-known chefs – fighting to stand out. And I said to George, 'It's not about dominating who you're with. They are looking for good interaction.' So in the audition, when he talked I listened; then when I talked, he listened. They kept calling us back in, and we were still there at the end of the day. I couldn't have been more pleased. That first whirlwind year on *MasterChef* brought us even closer.

What I love about George's food is that it goes from being creative, left of centre and ingenious to being honest and full of flavour. If George were a dish, I reckon he'd be plump little scallop loukoumades (deep-fried pastry balls) with proper Greek tarama, candied olives and something whacky that turns tradition upside down.

I now have so much more appreciation of a simple dish cooked in an unexpected way than a clever dish cooked in a technical, smarty-pants way. Recently on *MasterChef* George cooked lamb shanks with yoghurt. He covered the shanks with yoghurt, added shallots and thyme, drizzled them with honey and stuck it in the oven. Technically it was the antithesis of the way I was trained; twenty years ago I'd have said, 'You can't do a braise like that – you've got to colour the meat, and pass the sauce through a sieve.' But it was absolutely perfect – a classic, Greek-style family dish with a twist that made it very now. When he cooks food that appeals to the eye rather than the soul, I give him a nudge and say, 'Does that taste good? You can recreate the burger, but if it doesn't taste as good as the burger then there's no point.'

'GEORGE + I HAVE THIS CHEEKY FRIENDSHIP WHERE ANYTHING GOES'

I look at George now as a chef and a restaurateur and I aspire to be more like him. I admire his success. Maybe ten years ago he aspired to be more like me. I often feel embarrassed telling people that he was my apprentice because he is such a good chef, such a well-rounded restaurateur. I almost feel that I should be his protégé, because he's taken cooking and restaurants to another level. Some people might be jealous of that but I've never been jealous at all, because I know how hard he works to get what he wants.

George on Gary

Gary Mehigan is the most technically driven chef I've met. He knows how to make classic sauces better than the French do. You could pull out an old Escoffier cookbook and pick any sauce and he'd be able to tell you the ingredients. He has an extraordinary knowledge and a method or technique for doing everything, even if it's just a ricotta pancake.

But Gary also has an extraordinary ability to manage kitchens and staff. Plenty of chefs are amazing and talented and can make food look great but they've got no idea how to treat people, how to work in a team, or how to run a restaurant profitably. Gary is the whole package.

Walking into the Hotel Sofitel on my first day I was daunted. It was tough. It was the last phase of big hotel restaurants really being five-star and I was so lucky to be in that era. I learned discipline. I learned the basics: how to make a chicken stock and scramble eggs the right way, how to make classic sauces properly.

Gary put everything in perspective for me as a young cook. When I was a third-year apprentice I remember Gary telling me that I was going to cook at the hotel's Café La. I said I didn't want to go there, that I wanted to stay in the fine diner, Le Restaurant, where everyone aspired to work. Raymond Capaldi was Executive Chef at Hotel Sofitel, he was experimenting with molecular gastronomy and I wanted to be part of that. But Gary insisted that I work in Café La. And I was upset. It was a Saturday night, with Gary, me and another chef in the kitchen. I was going down like a bucket, and Gary just looked at me and said, 'What's wrong? You're whingeing about coming into Café La but you can't hold down the section.' At that point I realised why I needed to be there and I shut my mouth.

Lots of young chefs think it's a glamorous job. It's not. It's long days on your feet doing the same thing for hours. But if you can really understand that, then it clicks. Gary always told me that before you start a task, you've got to work out how you can do it efficiently and perfectly. I learned very quickly to

tell him if something went wrong in prep time and let him help me sort it out. If I hid it, he always found out.

I often say that I'm a bit of Raymond and a bit of Gary. Raymond was a visionary; what I learned from him at Fenix was to look at food in a different way. Gary was the opposite. He wanted to do good, flavoursome, wholesome food. He was still very respectful of what Ray was doing, but at Fenix on a Saturday night, Gary understood that what the customers really wanted were rib eye fillets with pont neuf potatoes and peppercorn sauce, rather than something left of centre.

I went to Fenix as a chef de partie (station chef in charge of one section) and within a year Gary and Raymond gave me the head chef position. I thought I was too young, but Gary disagreed. 'Age has nothing to do with this,' he told me. 'You'll do it and you'll succeed; you'll make lots of mistakes and that's fine. Because I'm here to back you up.'

At Reserve, after Fenix, I decided to continue in the molecular gastronomy genre, but I knew in my heart I wasn't cooking the food I really wanted to eat. I think my food lacked soul back then – it was a bit too much fanfare, a bit too much bravado. At the end of the day, it's just food – it's got to taste good and look amazing. Gary's food always does – it always has substance and soul, it's sit-back-and-hold-your-belly type of stuff. If he were a dish he'd be a daube of beef cheeks, with pommes mousseline made from seventy-five per cent butter, twenty per cent potato and five per cent milk, and it would be rich and flavoursome.

Today, with my food, I try to take a spoonful of Gary, a dash of what I learned from Raymond, and a good handful of my Greek Cypriot background so that every dish that I cook, or that my chefs cook, is a reflection of me.

'I always thought Gary and I were colleagues first then friends second, however, Gary is my mate more than anything else'

Recently when Gary had a nasty fall and I was pretty much the first one on the scene, I was really upset knowing that my friend was hurt. Gary is my mate first, and *MasterChef* has given us that. Gary always says he's not my mentor but he is. I'm proud of what he's taught me, and he should be too.

Anc

Ou

Nu

Ho

nt Grains

Chocolate

Saffron

Bread

ve Oil

Cheese

PROVIDORE

ts

Olives

Vanilla

Dried Beans

ey

Eggs

Flour

Rice

Ancient Grains

Freekeh and quinoa are the 'hit' grains of the last couple of years, which is great to see as they are tasty, textural and good for you. These tried and tested grains have been around long before the super-wheat cultivars of the modern era. That's not to say that there is anything wrong with modern wheat, unless of course you are a coeliac, but it's nice to enjoy a little variety. GARY

Ancient grains are very fashionable at the moment, which is a good thing as they're healthy and tasty and we should be eating more of them. It's great to see them appearing on a lot of my chef colleagues' menus. My mum comes from Cyprus and her cooking has always been heavily influenced by Middle Eastern ingredients and flavours so I grew up eating plenty of grains. Freekeh, dried green (or immature) wheat, is one of my favourite grains. The name comes from the Arabic word *farik*, which translates as 'rubbed'. The grain is dried and rubbed during its production to form nutty, chewy little pieces of goodness. George

FREEKEH WITH ROASTED PARSNIP AND HONEY

SERVES 4 AS A LIGHT LUNCH OR SIDE DISH

165 g cracked freekeh
(see page 266)
625 ml water
sea salt flakes and freshly ground
black pepper
3 parsnips, halved lengthways,
top portions quartered
2 tablespoons olive oil
1 red onion, cut into 8 wedges
3 sprigs thyme
25 g walnuts
½ teaspoon ground cumin
1 clove garlic, thinly sliced
½ teaspoon honey
finely grated zest and juice
of 1 lemon
125 ml extra virgin olive oil
95 g natural sheep's milk yoghurt
small handful of mache
(lamb's lettuce)

Freekeh has a lovely nutty flavour and slightly chewy texture when cooked correctly. I love roasted parsnips – they are sweet, earthy and, when sprinkled with a little cumin, go up more than a few notches in the must-eat-more-regulary stakes. All this salad needs is some creamy yoghurt and a scattering of mache to make it perfect. This makes a brilliant accompaniment to barbecued fish or chicken.

1 Place the freekeh and water in a small saucepan over high heat and bring to the boil. Reduce the heat to low, pop on a lid and simmer for 15 minutes or until all the water has been absorbed. Pop the lid back on and leave to cool. Transfer to a large bowl, season with a sprinkle of salt and pepper, stir well, then set aside.

2 Meanwhile, preheat a fan-forced oven to 180°C.

3 Remove the woody centre from the parsnips. Heat an ovenproof non-stick frying pan over medium heat, then add the oil, onion and parsnip and cook for 3–4 minutes or until light-golden brown on all sides. Scatter with the thyme, walnuts, cumin and half of the garlic, then season with a pinch of salt. Roast for 10 minutes or until golden, turning once. Remove from the oven and drizzle with the honey, then set aside.

4 Finely chop the remaining garlic and place in a small bowl with the lemon zest and juice. Whisk in the extra virgin olive oil and season with a pinch of salt and a few twists of black pepper.

5 Spread the sheep's milk yoghurt onto a large plate or 4 small plates. Sprinkle with the freekeh, drizzle with a little of the dressing and pile the parsnip, onion and walnuts on top. Scatter with the mache and drizzle with the remaining dressing, then serve.

'Tabbouleh' with preserved lemon

This is not your traditional tabbouleh as I use freekeh instead of burghul. The freekeh gives the dish a wonderful chewy texture. I ate this version of tabbouleh often as a child, spread on bread or toast. Eat it as a meal in itself with a dollop of yoghurt on top or serve it as a side dish for fish or pork.

1   Place freekeh and water in a saucepan and bring to a simmer over high heat. Reduce heat to low and cook until tender, approximately 50 minutes. Spread freekeh over a baking tray and set aside to cool.

2   Add parsley, coriander, raisins and preserved lemon to freekeh. Add lemon juice and olive oil, then season with sea salt. Stir to mix. Serve scattered with extra parsley sprigs.

SERVES 6 AS A SIDE DISH

250 g freekeh (see page 266)
1.3 litres water
½ cup finely chopped flat-leaf
   parsley, plus extra sprigs to serve
⅓ cup finely chopped coriander
40 g raisins
1 preserved lemon quarter
   (see page 140), pulp removed,
   rind finely chopped
juice of ½ lemon
80 ml extra virgin olive oil
sea salt flakes

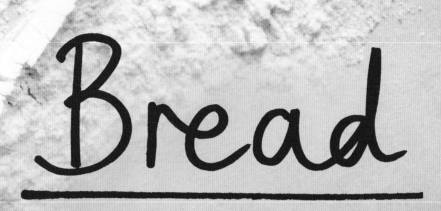

Bread

I love George's 'Day-old bread soaked in juices from a Greek salad' (see page 13). With a twinkle in his eye, he told me it was one of the best things he had eaten on a recent trip to Greece. What a brilliant way to make the most of leftovers. The funny thing is that it makes perfect sense – we all know the best bit of a salad, or many things come to think of it, are the juices and dregs at the bottom of the bowl, mopped up with bread. GARY

Breaking bread at the start of the meal symbolises sharing with family and friends, so bread should always be a part of your table. I have great memories of going back to my father's family village in Lemnos and walking down to the *forno* (wood-fired oven) to collect fresh, crusty bread. In Australia we often over-analyse bread. Usually I just want a nice, fresh crusty loaf. I don't need all the hoo-ha. *George*

FOCACCIA WITH CHILLI OIL

I have to admit I took a little advice on this focaccia from Lance Rosen, a chef from Rusk Restaurant in Melbourne. He has been a good friend for many years and loves making all of his own bread. Lance nurtures more than a few sourdough starters and gave me the 'bookfold' technique I use in this recipe to create a nice, open-textured, light bread. Ruffle the dough and create big unwieldy bubbles of air for a brilliant focaccia. Thanks Lance! Bear in mind that humidity and the ambient temperature affect how quickly yeast works so, depending on the weather, the dough may take more or less time than I've given here to prove.

SERVES 6

15 g dried yeast
275 ml water (36°C, just warm)
1 tablespoon caster sugar
500 g strong plain flour
  (see page 266)
10 g table salt
90 ml extra virgin olive oil
30 ml water
1 sprig rosemary, leaves picked
2 teaspoons sea salt flakes
125 ml thickened cream (optional)
100 ml olive oil
1 clove garlic, thinly sliced
⅓ cup chilli flakes

1   Place the yeast, warm water and half of the sugar in a bowl and stir to combine. Stand for 10 minutes or until foamy. Place the flour, salt and remaining sugar in a large bowl. Create a well in the centre of the flour and pour in the yeast mixture. Using your fingertips, draw the flour into the liquid and bring together to form a ball of soft, cohesive dough. Turn onto the bench and knead for 2–3 minutes or until smooth. Place onto a long baking tray (mine is 26 cm × 16 cm), press down with your fingertips to flatten slightly and tip 60 ml of the extra virgin olive oil over the dough. Leave to prove in a nice warm spot for 45 minutes or until it has doubled in size. Press down and stretch the dough to form a 50 cm × 30 cm rectangle, then fold one end into the centre and then the other end over the top of the folded portion, like a book fold. Leave dough to prove for another 45 minutes or until it doubles in size. Repeat this process of stretching, folding and proving one more time.

2   Mix the remaining 30 ml extra virgin olive oil with the 30 ml water. Spread the dough across the baking tray, ruffling the dough loosely to create uneven folds. Brush with the water and oil mixture, then sprinkle with the rosemary and salt and leave to prove in a warm spot for 30 minutes or until doubled in size.

3   Preheat a fan-forced oven to 220°C.

4   Bake the dough for 25 minutes or until light golden in colour. Pour on the cream (if using) and bake for a further 5 minutes at 200°C; this forms a rich, golden crust. Remove from the oven and leave to cool.

5   Meanwhile, warm the olive oil in a small saucepan so it is the same temperature as the hot water from your tap. Add the garlic and chilli. Set aside to infuse for 30 minutes.

6   Serve the garlic and chilli oil with the sliced focaccia for dipping.

Day-old bread soaked in juices from a Greek salad

This dish turns the Greek salad on its head as it's the dressing that contains the classic salad ingredients. Growing up, it was my father's right as head of the family to polish off the remains of the salad and mop up the delicious juices with a chunk of bread. (One day I might get that right, but there's another brother in front of me!) This is a bit of a chef's take on that flavour combination. You need to start the recipe a day ahead to drain out the salad juices.

1   Place yoghurt on a sheet of muslin, then wrap and suspend over a bowl in the fridge to drain for 8–12 hours to remove the liquid and make the yoghurt firm. Remove yoghurt from muslin, transfer to an airtight container and refrigerate until needed.

2   Blend tomato, onion, cucumber, basil, worcestershire and Tabasco in a food processor until a smooth puree forms.

3   Transfer puree to a clean muslin cloth, then wrap and hang in the fridge overnight over a bowl to collect any juices.

4   Next day, discard puree in cloth and reserve bowl of juices; this is the juice from a Greek salad for soaking the bread.

5   Remove crusts from bread loaf, keeping loaf whole.

6   Mix 200 ml Greek salad juice with yoghurt. Season to taste with sea salt.

7   Using your hands, break bread into small pieces, then transfer them to salad juice and yoghurt mixture and leave to soak for at least 10 minutes.

8   Serve soaked bread scattered with mint, parsley and oregano and drizzled with extra virgin olive oil.

SERVES 4 AS A STARTER

250 g natural Greek-style yoghurt
400 g over-ripe tomatoes, quartered, cored
¼ red onion, roughly chopped
1 lebanese cucumber, seeded, roughly chopped
5 basil leaves
½ teaspoon worcestershire sauce
2 drops Tabasco sauce
1 loaf day-old rustic bread (about 400 g)
sea salt flakes
5 sprigs mint, chopped
flat-leaf parsley leaves and oregano sprigs, to serve
extra virgin olive oil, for drizzling

cheese

Marooned on a desert island? I would have to take cheese:
a couple of soft and slightly smelly wine-washed cheeses; a nice
blue, preferably stilton; and a crumbly cheddar. I would most
probably wrap the cheese in banana leaves and bury it in the
cool sand in a flawed attempt to keep it going for as
long as I could. HELP! GARY

I'm particularly proud of top-quality Greek feta. A great
feta is a balanced blend of goat's milk and sheep's milk; too
often, in this country and elsewhere, inferior cow's milk is used. We
don't consume enough goat's milk in Australia – yet it's so good for
us and it makes feta taste amazing. There are loads of other Greek
cheeses. Think of just about any Italian cheese and there's usually
a Greek version of it, made in our own style, from barrel-aged
feta to kefalograviera, a hard sheep's milk cheese
similar to parmesan. George

TWICE-BAKED GRUYERE SOUFFLES

Gordon Ramsay might not know this, but I did a stage at Le Gavroche, the famous London restaurant owned by the Roux brothers, at the time when he was working his butt off there knocking out beautiful creamy and cheesy souffles served in tin-lined copper pans. Inspired by this signature Le Gavroche dish, these souffles (pictured over the page) are as irresistible now as they looked back then.

SERVES 4 AS A STARTER

60 g unsalted butter, plus
   20 g extra for greasing
25 g dried fine breadcrumbs
350 ml milk
pinch of grated nutmeg
table salt and freshly ground
   white pepper
40 g plain flour
150 g gruyere cheese, grated
6 free-range eggs, separated
200 ml thickened cream

1 Preheat a fan-forced oven to 180°C.

2 Butter four 250 ml-capacity round-bottomed ovenproof moulds with the extra 20 g butter, taking care to cover evenly, then refrigerate for 10 minutes. Butter the moulds again to ensure they are coated evenly. Place 1 tablespoonful of the breadcrumbs into each mould and turn to coat the insides evenly, then tip away any excess crumbs.

3 Bring the milk to the boil in a small saucepan over high heat. Add the nutmeg, a pinch of salt and a twist of pepper.

4 Meanwhile, melt the 60 g butter in a saucepan over medium heat and add the flour, then cook for a few minutes, stirring regularly. Remove from the heat and cool for a minute or two.

5 Return the cooled butter and flour mixture to medium heat and add the hot milk one ladleful at a time, mixing vigorously with a wooden spoon to combine all the ingredients. It is important to stir constantly while adding the milk to prevent lumps forming – make sure all the milk has been combined and the mixture is smooth before adding the next ladleful. Bring to a gentle simmer over low heat and cook for 3 minutes, then remove from the heat. Add half of the grated gruyere and the egg yolks, then stir to combine and transfer to a large bowl.

6 Using hand-held electric beaters, whip the egg whites and a pinch of salt in a clean bowl until soft peaks form. Gently fold one-third of the egg whites into the cheese sauce and combine, followed by the remaining whites, gently folding again to combine. Carefully spoon one-quarter of the mixture into each mould, taking care not to spill any on the rim of the moulds to ensure the mixture doesn't catch to the side of the mould as it rises. Fill to the top.

7 Bake the souffles for 12 minutes or until they have risen and are golden. Remove from the oven and cool. To gently release the souffles, use a tea towel to pick up a souffle mould in one hand and tip it gently on its side. Tip the souffle out into your other hand, then place it top-side up on a bench or baking tray.

8 Pour the cream into an ovenproof frying pan or deep baking dish just large enough to hold the souffles. Sprinkle half of the remaining cheese over the cream. Place the souffles in the cream and sprinkle the remaining cheese on top. Bake for 10 minutes or until golden brown, puffy and bubbly, then serve.

Baked feta souffles with smoked almond and grape vinaigrette

I've been classically trained so my food lends itself, in terms of technique, to French cooking. In this dish (pictured over the page) I've taken the humble cheese souffle and added a Greek touch with salty feta and a smoky almond and fruity grape vinaigrette, which you can spoon over the top or serve as a small side salad. With these souffles, it's not about the height but more about the texture. They should be crisp on the outside and soft and a little bit gooey (but not runny) in the centre.

1　Heat a splash of olive oil in a small frying pan, then saute onion and thyme over medium heat for 5–6 minutes or until soft. Blend with a stick blender.

2　Lightly grease six 250 ml-capacity souffle moulds with extra soft butter.

3　Heat milk in a saucepan over low heat; do not allow to boil.

4　Melt butter in another saucepan over medium heat, then add flour and cook, stirring, for 3 minutes. Gradually add hot milk, stirring well. Bring to the boil, then boil for 2 minutes. Add feta and combine well. Add onion mixture, then leave to cool slightly. Add egg yolks.

5　Preheat a fan-forced oven to 150°C.

6　Using a whisk, whisk egg whites to form soft peaks. Fold through cheese mixture. Fill moulds three-quarters full with cheese mixture. Place souffle moulds in a roasting pan, then fill pan three-quarters with boiling water. Carefully transfer pan with souffle moulds to oven. Bake for 25–30 minutes.

7　Meanwhile, for vinaigrette, place grapes and shallot in a mixing bowl, add tomato sauce, sherry vinegar, olive oil and sultanas and mix together well. Add almonds. Season with sea salt and set aside.

8　Serve souffles with smoked almond and grape vinaigrette spooned over and to the side and scattered with baby mache.

SERVES 6 AS A STARTER

olive oil, for cooking
1 small onion, finely chopped
1 teaspoon thyme, chopped
50 g unsalted butter, plus extra
　soft butter for greasing
300 ml milk
60 g plain flour
90 g feta, crumbled
3 free-range egg yolks
4 free-range egg whites

Smoked almond and grape vinaigrette
100 g red grapes, washed,
　halved lengthways
3 small shallots, finely chopped
1 tablespoon tomato sauce
1 tablespoon sherry vinegar
80 ml extra virgin olive oil
30 g sultanas
30 g smoked almonds, quartered
sea salt flakes
baby mache (lamb's lettuce),
　to serve

Chocolate

My wife, Mandy, always reads the menu at a restaurant all the way through, peering at the desserts and hoping there is a luscious, irresistible chocolate offering so she can sacrifice an entree or even a main to justify the indulgence – and my honeycomb recipe on page 23 fits the bill. Clever, clever girl! GARY

Good-quality dark chocolate has a high percentage of cocoa mass. The higher the percentage of cocoa, the fewer artificial flavours (such as refined sugar and milk solids) have to be added. A good, bitter dark chocolate that has savoury sweetness is heaven. Some chefs favour particular brands. I find that chocolate is a bit like wine. When people taste it they'll either like it or not. George

CHOCOLATE HONEYCOMB

Honeycomb is a staple at Fenix. We sell it by the bucketload over the bar with coffee or as a little sweet finish to a meal. We make it once every month, except during the height of summer when the humidity makes it too difficult. All the crumbly leftover bits are eaten by ravenous chefs or churned into ice cream for desserts. It is important to use a deep roasting pan because the bicarbonate of soda aerates the toffee and, as soon as it hits the mixture, it expands quickly, like lava. Hot molten toffee, like lava, is extremely dangerous. So have a go, but remember that working with boiling sugar is strictly out of bounds for kids. It is important to add the bicarbonate of soda to the pan as soon as the first tinges of brown appear, as the mixture browns very quickly.

SERVES 10

365 g caster sugar
170 g liquid glucose (see page 266)
110 ml water
1 tablespoon bicarbonate of soda
300 g dark or milk chocolate, chopped (or use buttons)

1   Line the base and sides of a 30 cm × 24 cm × 9 cm deep roasting pan with a large sheet of baking paper. Place the pan next to the stove.

2   Weigh the sugar into a bowl. Keeping the bowl on the scales, weigh the glucose, carefully pouring it on top of the sugar; this avoids unnecessary mess as glucose is very sticky and as a result can be difficult to transfer between containers. Slide the mixture into a deep, heavy-based saucepan (the one I use is 24 cm × 19 cm). Pour the water over the mixture and allow it to dissolve for a few minutes. Place over high heat for 4 minutes or until the sugar has dissolved into a syrup and the mixture is bubbling and thickened; use a pastry brush dipped in a little water to 'paint' the side of the pan occasionally to stop the sugar crystallising on the pan. As soon you see the first tinges of amber-brown appearing in the mixture, immediately sprinkle in the bicarbonate of soda. Whisk the bicarbonate of soda in quickly; as soon it hits the sugar it will foam up.

3   Quickly pour the mixture into the prepared tray, then scrape the pan around the edge once only. There will be some mixture left in the pan, but don't worry as this whole process needs to happen quickly to get beautiful, airy, bubbly honeycomb. Leave to set in a cool, airy spot on the bench-top for 30–40 minutes; it is important not to tap or move the honeycomb while it is soft as it may collapse. (To clean the pan of toffee, fill it with hot water and pop it onto the stove over low heat until the toffee dissolves, then wash.)

4   When the honeycomb has cooled and is brittle, lift it out using the paper.

5   Melt the chocolate in the microwave for 1 minute on high (or place in a double boiler over a pan of simmering water for several minutes) and stir until smooth.

6   Remove the paper and paint the honeycomb liberally with the melted chocolate. When the chocolate has set, gently break the honeycomb up into pieces with the back of a knife and serve.

Chocolate and mastic hotpot with 'Tsoureki'

SERVES 6–8

100 ml full-cream milk

400 ml pouring cream

300 g dark couverture chocolate buttons (55 per cent cocoa solids, see page 266)

4 drops mastic oil or 1 mastic bead, ground (see page 267)

'Tsoureki'

40 g fresh yeast

180 g caster sugar

200 ml milk, warmed

500 g strong plain flour (see page 266), plus extra for dusting

1 teaspoon table salt

4 drops mastic oil or 1 mastic bead, ground (see page 267)

10 g ground mahlep

2 free-range eggs

100 g soft unsalted butter, chopped

olive oil, for greasing

Mastic, a resin from trees found on the Greek island of Chios, adds an interesting wood-pine flavour to this rich hotpot. There are mastic shops all over Greece. The oil is difficult to find here, but mastic beads are available at good Mediterranean delis. You can substitute one mastic bead, ground up with a mortar and pestle, for the four drops of oil in the hotpot.

Tsoureki is a Greek brioche-like bread, usually eaten at Easter. (If there's any left over, store it in the freezer, then toast it for breakfast.) Mahlep, a spice made from ground kernels of a wild cherry, adds an anise–cinnamon flavour to the tsoureki.

1 For 'tsoureki', dissolve yeast and 1 teaspoon of sugar in warm milk. Add 150 g of the flour and stir to combine. Cover and stand in a warm place for 15 minutes or until it is spongey.

2 Place remaining flour and sugar, the salt, mastic and mahlep in the bowl of an electric mixer fitted with a dough hook. Add yeast mixture and 1 of the eggs and mix on low speed for 6 minutes. Gradually add butter, piece by piece, then beat until smooth. Place dough in an oiled bowl, cover with plastic film and leave in a warm place for 1½ hours or until doubled in size.

3 Knock back dough on a floured bench, then transfer to a greased 28 cm × 10 cm loaf tin. Cover tin with a damp tea towel and prove in a warm place for 30 minutes.

4 Preheat a fan-forced oven to 170°C.

5 Bake 'tsoureki' dough for 20 minutes. Beat remaining egg with a fork, then brush over top of dough. Bake for a further 15 minutes or until a skewer inserted in the centre comes out clean. Remove from loaf tin and leave to cool on a wire rack.

6 Heat milk and cream in a small saucepan; do not allow to boil. Place chocolate in a heatproof bowl, then pour in hot milk and cream mixture. Whisk until combined. Add mastic and stir.

7 Serve chocolate and mastic hotpot immediately with slices of 'tsoureki' to the side.

Dried Beans

We don't eat enough beans and pulses; they are an
excellent source of protein and fibre and are cheap to boot.
I love homemade baked beans, and find that borlotti or cannellini
beans are best. (As much as I love cooking with dried beans,
I do also like to use fresh borlotti beans when they are in
season — they are so pretty, bright and vibrant, it's a shame you
can't eat them raw as they lose colour and dull as they cook.
Can't have it all, eh?) GARY

The Mediterranean diet lends itself to lots of beans and pulses,
and dried beans are a traditional and common Greek ingredient.
Growing up we ate plenty of them — especially during Lent — and
I remember my mother cooking up big pots of giant beans braised
in tomato sauce or chick peas pounded up with garlic and
olive oil, served with crusty bread. George

GRILLED QUAIL WITH BRAISED CANNELLINI BEANS

Don't be scared of quail – they are in fact very quick and easy to cook and have a lovely flavour. This recipe allows you to make the beans in advance if you wish, then pop the quail on the barbecue for just long enough to add a little sizzle and smoke to each side. Best of all, quail are now available at larger supermarkets.

SERVES 4 AS A MAIN

8 quail
sea salt flakes and freshly ground
    white pepper
2 cloves garlic, thinly sliced
1 teaspoon rigani (mountain
    oregano, see page 267)
juice of 1 lemon
1 teaspoon chilli flakes
2 tablespoons extra virgin olive oil
lemon thyme sprigs (optional)
    and lemon wedges, to serve

Braised cannellini beans
100 g dried cannellini beans
4 vine-ripened tomatoes
boiling water
60 ml extra virgin olive oil, plus
    extra for drizzling
1 × 50 g piece smoked bacon,
    rind removed and discarded,
    cut into 5 mm dice
½ onion, finely chopped
2 cloves garlic, chopped
4 sprigs lemon thyme, plus
    extra to serve
1 tablespoon smoked paprika
    (see page 267)
2 tablespoons sherry vinegar
500 ml chicken stock
sea salt flakes

1 For the braised cannellini beans, soak the beans in a bowl of water for 5 hours. Drain and rinse, then set aside.

2 Cut a small cross on the base of the tomatoes, remove the cores and place tomatoes in a large heatproof bowl. Cover with boiling water and leave for 10 seconds. Drain and rinse tomatoes with cold water, then peel, remove the seeds and roughly chop. Set aside.

3 Heat 30 ml of the olive oil in a heavy-based saucepan for 30 seconds. Add the bacon, onion, garlic and thyme, then cook for 3–4 minutes until the onion has softened and the garlic and bacon are fragrant. Add the smoked paprika and cook for 2 minutes, stirring regularly. Add the vinegar, tomato and drained beans and stir to combine. Pour in the chicken stock and bring to the boil. Reduce the heat to low and simmer for 1 hour or until the beans are tender; the stock should have reduced by at least three-quarters. Add a good pinch of salt and the remaining olive oil, then leave to cool.

4 Meanwhile, preheat a barbecue grill-plate to high heat.

5 Split each quail down the back using a heavy knife or poultry scissors, then remove the backbone and flatten the quail, breast-side up. Place the quail in a large baking dish, then season with salt, pepper, garlic, rigani, lemon juice, chilli and extra virgin olive oil. Leave to stand for 5 minutes.

6 Barbecue the quail skin-side down for 3 minutes, then turn and cook for another 1 minute or until tender. Remove and leave to rest for 3 minutes.

7 Spread the braised beans over a large platter, then place the grilled quail on top, scatter with lemon thyme and serve with lemon wedges to the side.

chilli-salted beans

These days, I am not a big bean eater (they have a windy effect on many people!), but done like this they are absolutely delicious and you can't stop eating them. They go particularly well with beer – and Gary loves beer! Eat them instead of salted nuts with an aperitif and really get your tastebuds ready for a big dinner. Remember, don't salt the water when cooking beans as it will toughen the skins and they'll take longer to cook.

1   Soak dried beans together in cold water overnight.

2   Remove beans from water and place in a large saucepan, then cover with cold water. Bring to boil, then reduce heat to low and cook until tender, approximately 45 minutes; do not season during cooking. Season with sea salt, then cook for another minute.

3   Drain beans, then transfer to a baking tray lined with paper towel and place in fridge to dry for at least 2 hours.

4   Meanwhile, for spicy salt, mix together flour, cinnamon, cayenne pepper and salt.

5   Heat oil for deep-frying in a heavy-based saucepan until it registers 190°C on a candy thermometer. Working in small batches, dust dried beans with spicy salt and deep-fry for 2–3 minutes or until golden and crispy. Drain on paper towel. Sprinkle with a little sea salt. Serve immediately.

SERVES 4–6

50 g dried butter or borlotti beans
50 g dried black-eyed beans
50 g dried cannellini beans
50 g dried chick peas
sea salt flakes
vegetable oil, for deep-frying

Spicy salt
100 g plain flour
1 teaspoon ground cinnamon
2 teaspoons cayenne pepper
2 teaspoons table salt

Eggs

It is impossible to cook well without eggs, the perfect convenience food. We are finally learning, too, to treat our hens and poultry in general with greater respect – happy chickens and ducks mean tastier eggs. GARY

Where would we be without eggs? There's nothing better than a fresh egg and nothing worse than a stale one. Egg yolks have their own versatility and beauty; the whites as well. Eggs are the one ingredient that divides people into two camps – the healthy ones and those who want to indulge. Some people will only ever eat the white and others just love the creamy yolk and everything that can be made from it. George

SOFT-POACHED DUCK EGGS WITH POTATO, MUSHROOMS AND BLACK PUDDING

SERVES 4 AS A LIGHT MEAL

4 kipfler potatoes
2 king brown mushrooms
   (see page 267)
2 tablespoons extra virgin olive oil
sea salt flakes
4 duck eggs (or use hen eggs
   if unavailable)
60 ml olive oil
1 × 150 g black pudding, cut into
   1.5 cm-thick rounds
1 sprig thyme
1 tablespoon raspberry vinegar
freshly ground black or
   white pepper
flat-leaf parsley leaves, pale inner
   celery leaves and edible flowers
   (optional), to serve

Poached eggs, particularly poached duck eggs, make everything taste great. A slice of toast topped with a soft yielding egg with a gooey yolk sends shivers down my spine. This salad is like a big breakfast, but you can also have it for lunch or dinner. Warm, slightly waxy potatoes, soft black pudding and crisp celery leaves are all invited to the party and do the rumba with the egg.

1   Preheat a fan-forced oven to 180°C.

2   Place the potatoes in a small saucepan and cover with cold water. Bring to the boil and simmer for 15 minutes or until tender. When cool enough to handle, peel and cut into 1 cm-thick rounds, then set aside.

3   Meanwhile, cut the stems of the mushrooms into rounds and cut the caps in half. Set aside.

4   Assemble 4 small cups or bowls. Cut 4 pieces of plastic film that will sit comfortably inside the cups leaving 5 cm overhanging. Drizzle in a little extra virgin olive oil and crack an egg into each cup or bowl, then season with a pinch of salt. Gather the overhanging plastic film up to enclose the egg, lift out of the cup, then gently press with your fingers to expel any air. Twist the plastic film to tighten and shape the egg. Tie off the tops of the plastic film (or use kitchen string if preferred) to secure the eggs, then set aside. Bring a small saucepan filled three-quarters with water to the boil, then reduce the heat to low–medium.

5   Meanwhile, heat a non-stick frying pan over high heat and pour in 30 ml of the olive oil. Carefully fry the mushrooms and black pudding for 3 minutes until golden brown, then season with salt and add the thyme. Carefully turn over and cook for another 3 minutes or until golden brown. Remove the pan from the heat and transfer the mushrooms and black pudding to a plate with the potato, then leave the pan to stand for 30 seconds to allow the heat to drop. Add the raspberry vinegar to the pan and stir in the remaining extra virgin olive oil, then transfer to a small bowl and set aside; this will be the dressing.

6   Place the plastic film–wrapped eggs carefully into the pan of simmering water and poach for 6 minutes. Remove with a slotted spoon and snip the plastic film at the knots, then carefully remove each egg and season with salt and pepper.

7   Transfer the potato, mushrooms, black pudding and eggs to wide shallow bowls or plates. Spoon a little dressing over them, then scatter with the parsley, celery leaves and flowers (if using). Sprinkle with a little sea salt and pepper, then serve.

Broccoli and egg

This is a feisty little dish, so full of flavour, but it's quick and easy and you don't need to be a genius to cook it. Broccoli is such an underrated ingredient. It's high in vitamins and, with a few tweaks in the kitchen – in this case combining it with bacon, onion and herbs – it's absolutely delicious. The egg yolk is just warmed through under the griller immediately before serving. I think of this as a side dish; one perfectly matched with a grilled steak or pan-fried chicken livers.

1   Preheat a griller on high heat.

2   Heat olive oil in a heavy-based frying pan over medium–high heat. Add onion and cook for 6–8 minutes or until light golden.

3   Add bacon to pan and cook for 2–3 minutes. Add broccoli, then reduce heat to medium and cook, covered, for 3–4 minutes or until tender but still bright green and holding its shape. Add sherry vinegar. Remove from heat and stir through egg white, then season with pepper. Transfer to a small baking dish, place egg yolk in centre of broccoli mixture and grill for 1 minute or until yolk is warm but not set.

4   Scatter with mint and thyme (if using) and serve immediately.

SERVES 4 AS A SIDE DISH

50 ml olive oil
1 small onion, finely chopped
1 × 200 g piece eye bacon, rind removed and discarded, cut into 1 cm pieces
1 large head broccoli (about 500 g), cut into small florets
1 teaspoon sherry vinegar
1 free-range egg, separated
freshly ground white pepper
mint sprigs and thyme flowers (optional), to serve

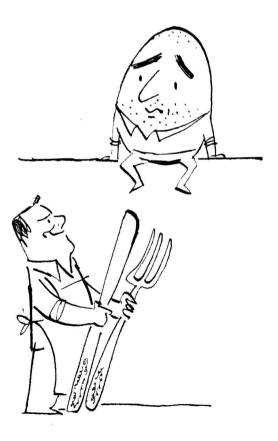

Flour

Where would we be without flour? Without breads of every description, pasta in all its glory, cakes, pastries and biscuits, to name but a few gems, we would have a very sad Gary and I think a very sad George! **GARY**

Understanding which flour to use for which sort of dish will help you obtain better results. For example, if you're making a delicate Genoese sponge then use a very light plain flour. For pasta, use an '00' flour (see page 266), which is very finely ground. While flour is prevalent in classic French dishes, especially pastries and tarts, it's not such a major ingredient in Greek cooking. At my restaurant Hellenic Republic we hardly use flour at all. *George*

PEANUT AND WHITE CHOCOLATE CHIP COOKIES

Everyone needs a nice cookie dough recipe that is gooey, totally irresistible and easy to keep in the fridge for those little moments when you get the munchies. Pop the oven on, plonk a few tablespoonfuls of dough onto a baking tray and bake – gee you're good!

1   Preheat a fan-forced oven to 180°C.

2   Using hand-held electric beaters, cream the butter and both sugars in a large bowl until pale, soft and fluffy. Add the egg and continue to mix until creamy. Stir in the flour, baking powder, chocolate and peanuts, mixing well. Turn dough out onto a bench lightly dusted with flour and knead for 30 seconds or so to ensure all the ingredients are fully incorporated.

3   Roll scant tablespoonfuls of the mixture into 2 cm balls, flatten them a little and place 3 cm apart on a large non-stick baking sheet. Bake for 10–12 minutes or until golden brown. Remove from the oven and leave to cool on the tray, if you have the willpower!

4   Store any leftover cookies in an airtight container for 2–3 days.

MAKES ABOUT 40

120 g soft unsalted butter, chopped
120 g caster sugar
120 g soft brown sugar
1 free-range egg
220 g plain flour
1 teaspoon baking powder
120 g good-quality white
    chocolate buttons
100 g salted roasted peanuts

Haloumi and mint ravioli with burnt butter and raisins

**SERVES 12 AS A STARTER
OR 4 AS A MAIN**

400 g haloumi cheese
  (see page 266)
200 g firm ricotta cheese
3 free-range eggs, 1 lightly beaten
10 mint leaves, finely shredded,
  plus extra leaves to serve
table salt
150 g unsalted butter, chopped
130 g raisins
130 g pistachios, toasted, peeled

Pasta dough
250 g strong plain flour ('00', see
  page 266), plus extra for dusting
2 × 55 g free-range eggs,
  lightly beaten
3 free-range egg yolks (from
  55 g eggs)
2 teaspoons extra virgin olive oil
semolina, for dusting

There's a certain sense of achievement when you make pasta, especially filled pasta. I've grown up eating loads of pasta of all shapes and sizes, even though my parents are of Greek and Cypriot heritage. I took this recipe from my mum, who would cook the ravioli in chicken broth and serve it in the stock finished with egg and lemon. My version is a lot richer than hers as I've topped the pasta with melted butter. She probably wouldn't eat it – she'd ask why I've used so much butter!

1   For pasta dough, pulse flour in a food processor for 30 seconds. While motor is running, add eggs, then egg yolks and olive oil. Keep processing until mixture reaches a coarse breadcrumb consistency. Shape into a ball, wrap with plastic film and leave to rest for 2 hours at room temperature.

2   Preheat a fan-forced oven to 190°C.

3   Bake haloumi on a baking tray for 20 minutes or until golden brown. Cool in fridge.

4   Finely grate haloumi into a mixing bowl. Add ricotta, the 2 unbeaten eggs and mint. Mix ingredients well, then divide into 12 balls (approximately 45 g each). Set aside.

5   Working on a surface lightly dusted with flour, cut pasta dough in half. Working with one piece at a time, feed dough through rollers of a pasta machine set at its widest setting, turning the handle and teasing the rolled dough along a bench as it feeds through the machine. Fold one end over onto centre and press it down. Fold other end over the top and press it down, then feed dough through machine using same setting. Repeat this process twice. Fold dough and feed it through the rollers, reducing the setting each time, making the dough thinner, until you reach the second last setting. Cut pasta sheet in half, then cover with a tea towel. Repeat with remaining dough to make 4 pasta sheets.

6   Take 1 sheet of pasta and put 6 balls of haloumi mixture in a row down centre, at 10 cm intervals. Lightly brush in between filling with beaten egg. Place another pasta sheet on top, press around filling to remove any air bubbles, then cut into 6 cm squares (if you want round ravioli then cut with a 6 cm pastry cutter). Place ravioli on a baking tray dusted with semolina. Repeat with remaining pasta sheets and filling.

7   Bring a large saucepan of water to the boil, then season with salt. Cook ravioli for 4 minutes or until they float to the surface. Remove with a slotted spoon to warm serving bowls.

8   Meanwhile, melt butter in a frying pan over high heat until it turns light brown, then add raisins and pistachios and pour over ravioli immediately. Scatter with extra mint leaves and serve at once.

Honey

I once worked in a restaurant where the honey man came to visit every week, bringing us a large box containing racks of waxy honeycomb bulging with fresh honey. He would collect the spent racks to reload into the hives and then bring them back to us with more honey. These memories are evocative and emotive, reminding me that honey is a special gift of nature. GARY

Honey is an amazing natural product that is good for you and sweet at the same time. When do we get something in life that is sweet and good for you? So eat it and enjoy it! I tend to cook with lots of honey, even in savoury dishes. I might finish a sauce with a teaspoon of honey just to elevate the flavour a bit. There are some great honeys being produced in Australia, especially in Tasmania. However, I particularly love honey from Attiki in Greece. The bees feed off thyme so you get an amazing savoury thyme flavour in the finished product. George

PANNA COTTA WITH ROASTED APRICOTS AND HONEY

SERVES 6

500 ml thickened cream
½ vanilla pod, split
60 g caster sugar
1½ leaves titanium-strength
    gelatine (see page 266)
olive oil, for greasing

Roasted apricots and honey
20 g unsalted butter
1 stick cinnamon
2 star anise
4 cloves
6 apricots, halved and stoned
dash of apricot liqueur
120 g honey

The secret to a good panna cotta (pictured over the page) is using the best-quality cream you can buy, then using just enough gelatine to hold it all together. As you turn out the panna cotta it should bow and bulge under its own weight. Soft, luscious and irresistible.

1 Place the cream, vanilla and sugar in a saucepan and bring to the boil, then remove from the heat. Meanwhile, soak the gelatine leaves in cold water until soft. Squeeze the leaves, then stir through the hot cream mixture until dissolved. Strain the liquid through a fine mesh sieve into a heatproof jug.

2 Oil six 100 ml-capacity dariole moulds very lightly with a little olive oil using the tip of your finger. Pour one-sixth of the cream mixture into each mould, then leave to set in the fridge for at least 6 hours or overnight.

3 Preheat a fan-forced oven to 180°C.

4 For the roasted apricots, place a heavy-based ovenproof frying pan over medium heat for 1 minute, then add the butter, cinnamon, star anise and cloves and allow the butter to melt and bubble. Place the apricots cut-side down into the pan and fry gently for 3–4 minutes or until golden. Turn the apricots over, then transfer the pan to the oven to roast for 4–5 minutes or until the apricots are just soft. Remove from the oven, then add the apricot liqueur and drizzle with the honey. Leave apricots to cool in the pan for 5–10 minutes.

5 To unmould the panna cotta, gently tease the edge of each dariole mould to release, then turn upside-down onto a bowl or plate. Place 2 apricot halves next to each panna cotta and drizzle with the syrup from the pan, then serve.

Rhubarb and 'melomakarona' crumble

Melomakarona are classic Greek honey biscuits, popular at Christmastime but also eaten year round. Somewhere between sweet and savoury, with a little bit of spice, they're like a Greek version of gingerbread. I like crumbling them over baked rhubarb for dessert (pictured over the page). Alternatively you can top rhubarb with the 'melomakarona' batter and bake it in the oven like a traditional fruit crumble.

1 Preheat a fan-forced oven to 140°C.

2 Place rhubarb in a roasting pan and cover with sugar, honey and water. Cover with foil and bake until soft and tender, approximately 25–30 minutes. Carefully drain liquid, then place rhubarb in a narrow 1 litre-capacity baking dish so it snuggly fits in 1 layer.

3 Meanwhile, for 'melomakarona' crumble, cream butter and icing sugar with hand-held electric beaters until pale and fluffy. Add olive oil, orange juice, cloves, nutmeg, walnuts, cinnamon and brandy. Mix well. Add flour and baking powder and beat until smooth.

4 Increase oven temperature to 170°C (fan-forced).

5 Place 'melomakarona' on a baking tray lined with baking paper. Using the palms of your hands, press mixture into a 1 cm-thick disc. Bake for 20–25 minutes or until golden. Remove from oven and set aside to cool.

6 Once 'melomakarona' crumble is cool, break up and scatter over rhubarb, then scatter with flaked almonds. Pop back in oven for 5 minutes or until just warm.

7 Serve immediately.

SERVES 4–6

12 stalks rhubarb, trimmed, washed, cut into 14 cm lengths
150 g caster sugar
150 g honey
150 ml water

'Melomakarona' crumble
50 g soft unsalted butter
20 g icing sugar
60 ml olive oil
2 tablespoons freshly squeezed orange juice
pinch of ground cloves
pinch of ground nutmeg
25 g ground walnuts, toasted, finely ground
¼ teaspoon ground cinnamon
2 teaspoons brandy
150 g plain flour
¼ teaspoon baking powder
2 tablespoons flaked almonds

Nuts

Walnuts remind me so much of Christmas. When I was little Santa would put a couple of tangerines and a few walnuts in the bottom of our stockings, which of course I never ate – chocolate is so much better when you are six! So when I think of nuts I think of that, and of standing on the sharp fragment of a walnut shell hidden in the red shag pile carpet – ouch! GARY

Forgetting flavour, nuts add an amazing textural element and natural oils to any food, and all cuisines around the world use nuts. The Chinese use peanuts, for example. I use a lot of pistachios and walnuts, which are grown in abundance in Greece, as well as pine nuts, which were regarded as an aphrodisiac in ancient Greece. I generally roast nuts before cooking with them. The only exception is in a couple of warm salads where I'll roast the ingredients and add raw nuts to them to add contrast to the dish. George

HAZELNUT, PISTACHIO AND CHERRY NOUGAT

Open a block of nougat and my willpower goes out the window. Jam-packed full of nuts and cherries, nougat is a little treasure chest of goodies suspended in a soft sticky pillow of gooeyness. It is surprisingly easy to make; you will, however, need a good electric mixer (mine is a KitchenAid) to complete the task, as trying to make it by hand would be a serious undertaking!

1   Preheat a fan-forced oven to 180°C.

2   Scald a clean mixing bowl (or the bowl of your electric mixer) with hot water. (Grease is the enemy and can stop egg whites from whipping perfectly. To prevent this, rinse the bowl with piping hot water and invert on the kitchen dish drainer to dry completely – don't dry with a tea towel as they can be greasy.)

3   Place the hazelnuts on a baking tray and bake for 6–8 minutes or until the skins are blistered and hazelnuts are golden. Remove from the oven and flip the hazelnuts into a clean tea towel. Wrap and then rub vigorously to remove the skins, then coarsely chop. Set the hazelnuts aside.

4   Bring the sugar and water slowly to the boil in a small saucepan, stirring over medium heat until the sugar dissolves and water begins to boil. Have a pastry brush in a small bowl of water on standby to brush down the inside of the pan every 3–4 minutes to prevent sugar crystals from forming as the syrup bubbles. This prevents the boiling sugar from crystallising.

5   Add the glucose and honey to the pan, then place a candy thermometer in the syrup. Continue to boil for 8 minutes or until the syrup reaches 147°C (hard-crack stage). Remove and set aside. (To test your sugar syrup without a candy thermometer, dip a teaspoon into the hot sugar syrup, then drop the syrup into a small bowl of water and it will set. It will reach soft-ball stage first, which means it will form a soft ball when you roll it between your fingers. When the sugar reaches hard-crack stage, a little piece of clear toffee will crack when broken between your fingers.)

6   Using hand-held electric beaters or an electric mixer with the whisk attachment on low speed, whisk the egg whites and a pinch of cream of tartar in the scalded and dried bowl until soft peaks form. Drizzle the hot sugar syrup in a fine stream down the side of the bowl into the egg whites, continuing to whisk the egg whites as you slowly pour. The egg whites will thicken and become heavy and glossy.

7   Working quickly, fold the hazelnuts, pistachios and glace cherries into the mixture and scrape it out onto one of the sheets of rice paper. Place the other sheet of rice paper on top and use a rolling pin to flatten the nougat, spreading it evenly between the rice paper; it should be 2 cm thick. Leave to set in a cool, airy place for at least 4 hours (but preferably overnight) before cutting.

MAKES 30 SMALL PIECES

65 g hazelnuts
375 g caster sugar
125 ml water
125 g liquid glucose (see page 266)
50 g honey
2 free-range egg whites,
   at room temperature
pinch of cream of tartar
65 g pistachios, chopped
65 g glace cherries, chopped
2 pieces confectionery rice paper
   (see page 267)

Chocolate, walnut and salty caramel tart

SERVES 8–10

110 g dark couverture chocolate
    (70 per cent cocoa solids,
    see page 266), chopped
40 g cold unsalted butter, chopped
125 ml thickened cream
2 teaspoons liquid glucose
    (see page 266)

Sweet pastry
300 g soft unsalted butter, chopped
150 g caster sugar
½ vanilla pod, seeds scraped
450 g plain flour, plus extra
    for dusting
1 free-range egg, lightly beaten
1 tablespoon thickened cream

Walnut praline
100 g walnuts
110 g caster sugar

Salty caramel sauce
200 ml pouring cream
180 g liquid glucose (see page 266)
180 g caster sugar
2 teaspoons sea salt flakes
180 g unsalted butter, chopped

This is my version of a Snickers bar, but instead of peanuts I use walnuts. It's important to toast or roast the nuts before using them. You could substitute macadamia nuts for walnuts in this recipe. It's slightly fiddly with lots of steps but the result is a decadently rich, salty caramel tart. Let the tart come to room temperature before you eat it. I reckon Gary and I could finish the entire tart – all Gary would need to be completely happy is a pot of tea.

1   For pastry, place butter, sugar and vanilla seeds in the bowl of an electric mixer fitted with a beater attachment and incorporate on lowest speed. Beat until smooth and creamy but not light and fluffy; do not cream too much. Add flour, egg and cream and mix until a smooth paste forms and mixture just comes together in a ball; take care not to overwork. Shape dough into a disc, divide in half, then wrap one half in plastic film and freeze for later use. Wrap the other half in plastic film and refrigerate for 1 hour.

2   Preheat a fan-forced oven to 160°C. For walnut praline, place walnuts on a baking tray and bake for 6–8 minutes or until lightly toasted. Remove and wrap in a clean tea towel, then rub to remove as much of skins as possible and place on a baking tray. Heat sugar in a heavy-based saucepan over low heat, without stirring but tilting the pan occasionally, for 10 minutes or until a dark but not burnt caramel forms. Pour caramel over nuts; make sure you cover each nut. Set aside to cool. Once set, break praline into a tea towel lined with baking paper and smash with a rolling pin until coarsely crushed. Set aside.

3   Roll dough between 2 sheets of baking paper until 5 mm thick. Line a shallow 24 cm tart tin with a removable base with pastry, trimming off excess. Refrigerate for 30 minutes.

4   Preheat a fan-forced oven to 170°C.

5   Line pastry shell with baking paper and top with pastry weights or dried beans. Blind bake pastry for 15 minutes or until dry. Remove baking paper and pastry weights or beans, reduce heat to 160°C and bake for another 10 minutes or until golden and dry.

6   Meanwhile, for salty caramel sauce, bring cream to the boil in a small saucepan over medium–high heat. Place glucose, sugar, salt and butter in another saucepan and heat over medium heat until glucose mixture registers 147°C on a candy thermometer, stirring occasionally to prevent sauce from catching. Add hot cream to glucose mixture and stir over low heat until incorporated. Remove from heat. Set aside until just warm.

7   Put chocolate and butter into a heatproof bowl. Bring cream and glucose to the boil in a small saucepan over medium heat. Pour over chocolate and butter, stand for 5 minutes, then stir until melted and smooth.

8   Sprinkle walnut praline over cooled pastry shell, then cover with a layer of caramel sauce. Leave for a few minutes, then pour chocolate mixture over caramel sauce so it reaches the top of the tin. Refrigerate for 1 hour or until chocolate mixture is firm. Serve at room temperature.

Olive Oil

I am not sure what I would do without olive oil; it seems
to be the one extravagance I can get away with. Like the grape,
the olive is a precious fruit that gives us a depth and variety
of flavours that keep even the fussiest cooks and
connoisseurs very happy indeed. GARY

Where would the world be without olive oil? I use Greek olive
oil, sent in barrels directly from a producer in Crete. There are
constant arguments about which country makes the best olive oil,
but the fact is that countries such as Spain, Italy and Greece have
had olive groves for centuries. I use an imported olive oil because
I like an intensely flavoured oil that's not grassy and green. Olive oil
is there to transport the other flavours through your palate, not
to overpower the food. The main rule with olive oil is to use
it regularly. Don't try to save it, bringing it out only for
a special occasion, or it will go rancid. George

PRAWN OIL

I have to give credit to Greg Brown for the idea of prawn oil. He was one of Australia's pre-eminent chefs back in the 90s. However, I have embellished it a little; this comes and goes on my menus in all sorts of guises and it is such a good larder standby for a quick pasta sauce or to use as a seasoning to tickle up a nice piece of fish on the barbecue. This not only makes lovely dressings for salads, but it also works well as a finishing touch for seafood-based pastas or risottos too.

MAKES 300 ML

500 ml olive oil
250 g prawns shells (from
    500 g raw prawns)
1 small carrot, finely chopped
1 small onion, finely chopped
½ bulb fennel, trimmed,
    finely chopped
2 star anise
1 teaspoon coriander seeds
1 teaspoon fennel seeds
2 sprigs thyme
3 coriander roots, well washed,
    roughly chopped
2 fresh bay leaves
50 ml brandy
20 ml Pernod
50 g tomato paste

1   Preheat a fan-forced oven to 160°C.

2   Heat a non-stick, ovenproof frying pan over high heat and pour in 2 tablespoons of the olive oil, then add the prawn shells. Fry the prawn shells for 4–5 minutes until they are light-golden brown. Transfer the pan to the oven to roast for 10 minutes, then remove and set aside.

3   Heat another 2 tablespoons of the olive oil in a heavy-based saucepan over medium heat, then add the carrot, onion and fennel and cook for 3–4 minutes or until golden. Add the prawn shells, star anise, coriander seeds and fennel seeds. Cook for 2 minutes, then add the thyme, coriander roots and bay leaves. Cook for a further 2 minutes. Add the brandy and Pernod and cook for 30 seconds. Add the tomato paste and cook for 2–3 minutes, stirring regularly. Cover with the remaining olive oil, then turn the heat down to low and simmer for 20 minutes, skimming the froth from the surface every 5 minutes.

4   Remove from the heat, then leave to cool. Strain through a fine mesh sieve into an airtight jar or container, then seal and store in the fridge for up to 1 month.

chocolate olive oil mousse

I stole this gorgeous recipe from Stelios, a very close friend of mine and an amazing pastry chef based in Athens. He came to Australia and did a dinner at The Press Club as part of the Melbourne Food and Wine Festival one year. There are only three simple ingredients here – chocolate, olive oil and whipped cream. No eggs, no flour. Make this and eat it straight away – don't put it in the fridge.

1 Gently melt chocolate in a heatproof bowl over a saucepan of simmering water, making sure base of pan does not touch water.

2 Remove bowl of melted chocolate from heat and stir in olive oil. Set aside.

3 Using a whisk, whip cream to form soft peaks. Add cream to melted chocolate and olive oil, then gently fold to mix well.

4 Serve immediately.

SERVES 6

100 g dark couverture chocolate
   (55 per cent cocoa solids,
   see page 266), chopped
50 g dark couverture chocolate
   (70 per cent cocoa solids,
   see page 266), chopped
100 ml extra virgin olive oil
250 ml double cream

Olives

Olives weren't the sort of thing we had in our house when
I was growing up; we were a very traditionally English family and
Mum was a conservative cook. My first introduction to these little
gems was via a friend who went to Spain on holiday and brought
back some lovely plump green olives that were succulent, grassy
and sweet. I also get a nice crop of my own from the two maturing
manzanilla and arbequina olive trees in my garden. GARY

Olive trees cover something like sixty per cent of the land
in Greece and I can tell you I have tasted a banquet of different
olives in my time. The most popular table olive is the kalamata.
It's simple, with good bitterness, and lots of flesh around the stone.
Occasionally I add chopped green olive to some of my sauces.
Green olives are a bit more acidic and a little bit more tangy than,
say, a Ligurian olive. One of the most important things to remember
is that olives need to be stored in olive oil to make sure
they retain their flavour. George

SWORDFISH WITH IRANIAN FIGS AND GREEN OLIVES

While I love all sorts of olives, I have a soft spot for the big green Sicilian olives, which I have used here as they go brilliantly with the dried figs and a nice piece of swordfish.

1   Place the figs in a small bowl and cover with boiling water. Leave to stand for 10 minutes, then drain, discarding the water. Pat the figs dry with paper towel, then cut into quarters and set aside.

2   Heat a small saucepan over medium heat, then add 1 tablespoon of the extra virgin olive oil. Cook the shallot and garlic for 2 minutes, stirring regularly; do not allow them to colour. Add the wine and figs, then increase the heat to high and reduce the wine by three-quarters. Remove from the heat and add the olives, remaining extra virgin olive oil and caperberries, then stir to mix. Leave to cool for 5 minutes. Season to taste with salt and a twist or two of pepper. Add the parsley, then stir and set aside.

3   Heat a heavy-based non-stick or enamelled cast-iron frying pan over high heat and add the olive oil. Season the swordfish steaks with salt and pepper, then pan-fry for 2–3 minutes (depending on their thickness) on each side or until tinged a light-golden brown; they are best cooked medium–rare. Remove from the pan and rest for 2 minutes.

4   Place the swordfish steaks on 4 plates, then spoon over the fig and olive mixture. Divide the lemon among the pieces of fish. Drizzle with a little vino cotto and serve immediately.

SERVES 4 AS A MAIN

95 g dried Iranian figs
boiling water
80 ml extra virgin olive oil
1 shallot, thinly sliced
½ clove garlic, sliced
250 ml dry white wine
60 g green Sicilian olives
80 g small caperberries
    (see page 266)
sea salt and freshly ground
    black pepper
1 cup flat-leaf parsley leaves,
    coarsely chopped
2 tablespoons olive oil
4 x 120 g swordfish steaks
sea salt and freshly ground
    black pepper
1 lemon, very thinly sliced
fig vino cotto (see page 267),
    for drizzling

carrot cake with black olive caramel

SERVES 8

2 free-range eggs
250 g soft brown sugar
150 ml extra virgin olive oil
1 teaspoon baking powder
200 g plain flour
¼ teaspoon bicarbonate of soda
½ teaspoon ground cloves
340 g grated carrot (about 5 carrots)
100 g sultanas
75 g walnuts, roughly chopped
double cream, to serve
olive leaves (optional), to garnish

Black olive caramel
200 g caster sugar
50 g liquid glucose (see page 266)
100 g black olive paste
  (see opposite)

Most people think you can only use olives in savoury dishes, however, the olive caramel is great with this sweet carrot cake and is also lovely with cheese as well. The inspiration for this came from the humble Aussie carrot cake, the type of cake my family's neighbours would bake to bring over to our house. I started thinking about how I could add my ideas to it. Olives and carrots work really well together; just add a little bit of sweetness and you've got a really nice savoury dessert. The saltiness of the olive paste really elevates the caramel. Black olive paste is available from good delis and larger supermarkets – don't confuse it with tapenade, which includes garlic and other seasonings.

1 Preheat a fan-forced oven to 160°C.

2 Place eggs and sugar in bowl of an electric mixer fitted with a paddle attachment and incorporate. Gradually add oil while continuing to beat. Fold in baking powder, flour, bicarbonate of soda, cloves, carrot, sultanas and walnuts.

3 Pour batter into a baking paper lined 30 cm × 20 cm slab tin and bake for 40 minutes or until a skewer inserted in centre comes out clean.

4 Meanwhile, for black olive caramel, place sugar and glucose in a saucepan over medium–high heat and cook until light-golden brown, approximately 5 minutes. Remove from heat and cool slightly. Whisk in olive paste, tilting pan occasionally and whisking continuously. Strain through a fine mesh sieve into a bowl. Keep warm.

5 Serve slices of carrot cake with spoonfuls of warm black olive caramel and double cream alongside. I like to garnish this with olive leaves, however, this is optional.

Rice

When I was growing up I must confess I thought that rice was just rice. The most exotic variety available at the time was Uncle Ben's polished rice – impossible to overcook and it never ever stuck. Now I know better! Three-quarters of the world relies on rice as its starch staple. Basmati, patna, jasmine, sticky, black, japonica, carnaroli, arborio, calasparra – take your pick! GARY

When we think of an ingredient that is universal, that we all use and love, it would have to be rice. When I think of rice I think of beautiful stews, great curries – above all, it's got to carry flavour. In my restaurants we might braise off a shoulder of lamb and tip in some short-grain rice at the end of cooking to soak up all the juices and flavours. Rice can also be the star of a dish, such as a simple risotto made with lots of love (see my Rabbit and Rosemary Risotto on page 215). Rice behaves in certain ways when you cook it and it's one of the most common things that people get wrong, in cafes, restaurants and homes. George

SAFFRON RISOTTO WITH CLAMS AND LEMON MASCARPONE

If you are looking for the perfect mid-week meal in a bowl, then risotto hits the spot. Why not try a really top-notch risotto rice – a seemingly expensive bag of carnaroli or vialone nano might seem extravagant at first, but, you only need a handful per person at the most.

SERVES 4 AS A MAIN

500 g clams or pipis, soaked in cold water to expel sand, washed well
60 ml olive oil
2 cloves garlic, finely chopped
1 onion, finely chopped
4 sprigs thyme
200 ml dry white wine
500 ml chicken stock, approximately
90 g unsalted butter, chopped
sea salt flakes
200 g risotto rice, such as carnaroli
2 good pinches of saffron threads
2 tablespoons mascarpone
2 tablespoons thickened cream
freshly ground white pepper
grated zest of ½ lemon
¼ cup flat-leaf parsley, chopped
extra virgin olive oil, to serve
thyme leaves and flowers (optional), to serve

1   Place a large stainless-steel saucepan with a lid over high heat and heat for 1 minute.

2   Meanwhile, drain the clams. Remove the lid from the pan and add 1 tablespoon of the olive oil. Add half of the garlic and onion. Quickly add the clams and thyme, stir once, then add 100 ml of the white wine and pop on the lid. Cook for 2–3 minutes or until the clams have popped open. Remove from the heat and drain in a colander with a bowl underneath to catch all the juices. Set the juices aside. Leave the clams to cool for a few minutes, then pick the meat from three-quarters of the shells and set aside. Discard the empty shells, onion, garlic and thyme.

3   Place the stock and the reserved shellfish juices in a large saucepan over high heat and bring to the boil. Melt 30 g of the butter in a wide, low non-stick saucepan over medium heat and cook the remaining garlic and onion for 2–3 minutes or until translucent, then add 1 teaspoon salt. Add the rice and cook over low heat for 2–3 minutes. Add the saffron and stir through the rice, then pour in the remaining white wine and stir for 1–2 minutes until reduced by half. Add three-quarters of the hot stock all at once and bring the rice to a simmer; avoid stirring too often. The stock should be absorbed gradually – it usually takes 15 minutes.

4   Meanwhile, place the mascarpone and cream in a small stainless-steel bowl, add a pinch of sea salt and a twist of white pepper, then add the lemon zest and whisk for 30 seconds until soft peaks form. Set aside.

5   As the stock is absorbed into the rice stir in the remaining stock, if required, until you have a soft yielding risotto with a tiny amount of bite to the grain. Add the remaining butter in small pieces and stir to incorporate. Add the clams in the shell and clam meat to the risotto and stir through gently. Turn the heat off and leave to sit for a minute for the heat to draw through the clams. Stir in the mascarpone mixture at the last second, along with the parsley.

6   Spoon onto plates, tapping to flatten a little. Drizzle with extra virgin olive oil, scatter with thyme leaves and flowers (if using) and serve.

'Habibi' rice

I got this recipe from Shane Delia, my mate and business partner at Melbourne restaurant Maha. That's why I named this dish 'habibi' rice (*habibi* means 'mate' in Arabic). Shane's of Maltese/Lebanese background, with a great command of Middle Eastern cooking, so 'habibi' seemed to fit here. Serve this delicious and aromatic rice dish with stews or casseroles or eat it the next day with yoghurt mixed through it as a salad.

1   Preheat a fan-forced oven to 180°C.

2   Place coriander and cumin seeds on a baking tray and roast for 5 minutes or until fragrant. Crush with a mortar and pestle.

3   Reduce oven temperature to 160°C. Place pine nuts and almonds on baking tray and roast for 7–10 minutes or until light golden.

4   Heat clarified butter in a frying pan over medium heat, then break in angel hair pasta in 1 cm lengths and fry until golden brown, approximately 2 minutes. Add onion and rice and cook until rice starts to absorb butter and onion begins to soften, approximately 5 minutes.

5   Add spices, nuts and water and bring to the boil. Cover and cook over low heat until water has been absorbed and rice is tender, approximately 10–12 minutes. Remove from heat and stand for 5 minutes.

6   Fluff with a fork, stir in sea salt to taste and serve immediately.

SERVES 6–8 AS A SIDE DISH

1 tablespoon coriander seeds
1 tablespoon cumin seeds
50 g pine nuts
50 g flaked almonds
100 g clarified butter (see page 266)
50 g angel hair pasta
½ onion, finely diced
250 g basmati rice, washed
750 ml hot water
sea salt flakes

Saffron

Wars were fought over this precious commodity – things
don't change, do they? It is still very expensive but adds an
intangible flavour and balance to a dish – the taste of the sun,
of Spain, Morocco and the Far East, all in the stamens
of the crocus flower. **GARY**

Having spent some time in Kozani, Greece (where I get my saffron
from for my restaurants), and seen first-hand how hard it is to
harvest – handpicking the stamens from the flower – I have so
much respect for this beautiful ingredient. The saffron I use is
aromatic, pungent and flavoursome. You only need a couple of
threads to achieve fabulous flavour. *George*

ESCABECHE OF MACKEREL

This dish can be prepared a day in advance and popped into the fridge until required. The flavours of the vinaigrette and saffron infuse beautifully with the fish. Ideally, serve this delicate yet tasty starter or light lunch with good-quality bread or boiled and peeled new potatoes to counteract the acidity of the fish, then offer a fresh salad to provide a little crunch. This is an ideal dish to place in the centre of your table to share.

1   Lightly crush the coriander and fennel seeds with a mortar and pestle and set aside.

2   Heat a small saucepan over low heat, then add 30 ml of the extra virgin olive oil. Cook the shallot and carrot for 2 minutes; do not allow to colour. Add the coriander seeds, fennel seeds, saffron and star anise and cook for a further 30 seconds. Pour in the vinegar and reduce by half. Add the white wine and reduce by half, then add the orange juice and remove from the heat. Add ½ teaspoon salt and the remaining extra virgin olive oil, then stir and set aside.

3   Heat a non-stick frying pan over medium heat and add the olive oil. Season the fish lightly with salt and pan-fry, skin-side down, for 2–3 minutes. Flip the fish over and cook for a further 2 minutes, then remove from the pan. Transfer the fish to a deep platter. Smother the fish with the fragrant vinegar mixture, scatter with the coriander leaves and leave to stand for at least 10–15 minutes to allow the flavours to develop. Serve at once.

SERVES 4 AS A STARTER OR LIGHT LUNCH

½ teaspoon coriander seeds
¼ teaspoon fennel seeds
100 ml extra virgin olive oil
2 small shallots, thinly sliced
1 carrot, sliced
2 pinches saffron threads
4 star anise
1½ tablespoons champagne vinegar
1½ tablespoons dry white wine
125 ml freshly squeezed
    orange juice
sea salt flakes
2 tablespoons olive oil
4 × 120 g mackerel fillets, skin-on,
    pin-boned
¼ cup coriander leaves

Roasted snapper with saffron-roasted peaches

The saffron in this dish is aromatic and almost floral. It imparts a distinct flavour, and is definitely the hero, not overpowered by either the snapper or the fruit. In the Byzantine era the Romans, Greeks and Persians didn't eat many carbs, but they used a lot of stone fruit in cooking. Peaches go really well with fish, and it doesn't matter if they are a little under-ripe.

SERVES 2 AS A MAIN

3 peaches, stoned and cut
   into eighths
pinch of saffron threads
1 vanilla pod, split
125 ml extra virgin olive oil
sea salt flakes
1 × 900 g snapper, cleaned, scaled
1 small lemon, thinly sliced
1 bulb fennel, trimmed, sliced
50 g unsalted butter, chopped
2 tablespoons chopped thyme
mint sprigs, to serve

1 Preheat a fan-forced oven to 180°C.

2 Place peaches in a roasting pan, then scatter with saffron and vanilla. Pour 60 ml of the olive oil evenly over peaches. Using your hands, mix peaches well, making sure saffron and vanilla are mixed through. Season with salt and bake for 10 minutes; peaches should still have a very slight crunch to them.

3 Take snapper and season with salt. Place lemon, fennel and 25 g of the butter inside cavity of snapper. Transfer snapper to a roasting pan. Drizzle remaining olive oil over snapper and scatter with thyme, then top with remaining butter. Bake for 20 minutes or until just cooked through.

4 Remove snapper from oven, scatter with mint, if desired, and serve with roasted peaches.

Vanilla

Last year I met Russell Spanton from Vanilla Australia, a passionate grower of vanilla in Australia's Far North. Like the hands of a car mechanic, his were a little stained and clearly belonged to someone who works with his hands. It turns out that vanilla needs a lot of love — not only is each plant pollinated by hand, but it also needs to be aged and turned and massaged along its length to ensure the even distribution of seeds. What fragrant hands Russell must have! GARY

Vanilla imparts a wonderful flavour and aroma to so many dishes. When you know what goes into growing and harvesting the pods, which are individually picked by hand, you will never waste a scrap. In Australia we are now harvesting vanilla grown in Queensland, which is extremely exciting. George

POACHED PEACHES WITH VIN SANTO AND VANILLA ICE CREAM

Peaches can be difficult to peel, so choose ripe peaches that are not too soft for the best chance of success. Vin Santo is an Italian dessert wine which, literally translated, means holy wine. Available from good bottle shops, it can usually be substituted with a good-quality dessert wine. Home-churned ice cream becomes harder over a number of days and may need to be tempered (allowed to soften) in the fridge for up to thirty minutes before serving. Remember, soft ice cream is the best!

1   For the vanilla ice cream, have two bowls ready, one a little larger than the other. Place the ice into the larger bowl. Have a fine mesh sieve handy. Bring the cream, milk, glucose and vanilla seeds and pod to the boil in a heavy-based saucepan over high heat.

2   In the smaller bowl, whisk the egg yolks and sugar until pale and fluffy. Immediately pour half of the hot cream mixture into the egg mixture and whisk to combine, then quickly return the egg mixture to the pan with the remaining hot cream mixture.

3   Place the empty bowl over the ice. Turn the heat to low and whisk the cream mixture until it registers 82°C on a candy thermometer; this takes approximately 2 minutes. If you do not have a candy thermometer, stir the mixture with a wooden spoon then, as the custard heats and thickens, lift out the spoon and wipe the back of it with your finger; there should be a clear track that does not move. Pour the custard immediately through a fine mesh sieve into the bowl sitting over the ice.

4   Whisk the custard 2–3 times quickly to remove some heat. Leave it to cool over the ice until completely cold, stirring occasionally. Pour the cold custard into an ice cream machine and churn according to the manufacturer's instructions. Makes 1 litre. This ice cream is best eaten within 3 days. It will keep for up to 1 month in the freezer, but will harden the longer it is kept.

5   Bring a large saucepan of water to the boil. Cut a cross in the base of the peaches with a paring knife, then place in the pan of boiling water for 30 seconds. Remove the peaches with a slotted spoon and refresh in a bowl of ice-cold water, then peel and set aside.

6   Place the vanilla pod and seeds, cinnamon, star anise, cloves, water, sugar and wine in a saucepan large enough to hold the peaches. Use a small whisk to distribute the seeds and allow the sugar to dissolve over low heat, still whisking, for 2–3 minutes.

7   Place the peaches in the warm sugar syrup; the syrup should just cover the peaches. Top the peaches with a small piece of baking paper cut to fit the pan; this keeps the heat and steam in the pan. Bring to the boil over high heat, then simmer over low heat for 15–20 minutes; the cooking time will depend on the size and ripeness of the peaches. Insert a paring knife into a peach and if there is no resistance, they are ready. Remove the pan from the heat and leave the peaches to cool in the syrup.

8   Divide the peaches among 4 bowls. Spoon about 100 ml of the poaching syrup into each bowl. Serve with spoonfuls of vanilla ice cream.

SERVES 4

8 small yellow or white peaches
ice cubes
1 vanilla pod, split, seeds scraped
1 stick cinnamon
2 star anise
2 cloves
450 ml water
150 g caster sugar
150 ml vin santo (Italian
   dessert wine)

Vanilla Ice Cream
crushed ice
500 ml thickened cream
500 ml milk
75 g liquid glucose (see page 266)
1 vanilla pod, split, seeds scraped
12 free-range egg yolks
100 g caster sugar

Strawberries and vanilla cooked in a bag

SERVES 2

250 g strawberries
1 vanilla pod, split, seeds scraped
1 tablespoon icing sugar
1 stick cinnamon
clotted cream and oregano leaves
   (optional), to serve

This dish is incredibly easy. You can prepare the strawberries in the paper parcel well in advance so all you have to do is cook them when you're ready. The gentle heat brings out the flavour of the strawberries and infuses the vanilla through them. Make sure when you wash the strawberries that you don't drown them in water or they will lose their flavour.

1   Preheat a fan-forced oven to 170°C.

2   Cut a 30 cm square piece of baking paper. Place strawberries in middle of paper. Scatter vanilla seeds and pod evenly over strawberries. Sprinkle sugar evenly over strawberries, then toss to coat. Add cinnamon, then bring together 4 corners of the paper and tie together with kitchen string so the parcel resembles a money bag. Bake for 12 minutes.

3   Open the bag, scatter with oregano leaves (if using) and serve strawberries with clotted cream to the side.

Be

B

Mush

Lett

auliflower

Eggplant

ries

Fennel

ans

Figs

Asparagus

_____

GREENGROCER

_____

ooms

Beetroot

Stone Fruit

Tomatoes

Lemons

uce

Onions

Potatoes

Asparagus

When I think of asparagus I think of spring and the first of the season's beautiful vegetables. Spring is a season full of my favourite things: peas, broad beans, the very first flush of early summer fruits and, of course, the warm weather. Ask me to name my favourite asparagus dish and I will give you twenty! GARY

Asparagus is an elegant, good-looking vegetable that can be used in so many ways. Shave it finely to make a salad, roast it simply with thyme, olive oil and sea salt or use it in a savoury custard. It makes a great side dish as well as a great meal. We only get a very short season for asparagus during spring so I believe we should overdose on it when the opportunity arises. Personally, I prefer to roast asparagus rather than boil it as I think it retains its true flavour better. George

ASPARAGUS WITH GOAT'S CURD AND GREEN OLIVE TAPENADE

I love using green and white asparagus together. In this recipe (pictured over the page) I've combined them with lemon and goat's cheese, which pair beautifully. The candied walnuts add a lovely earthiness and sweet crunch; little surprises that make this the perfect warm-weather salad. White anchovy fillets are anchovy fillets that have been marinated in vinegar.

SERVES 2 AS A STARTER

table salt
1 bunch green asparagus
1 bunch white asparagus
ice cubes
1 teaspoon honey
1 teaspoon dijon mustard
finely grated zest and juice
   of 1 lemon
60 ml extra virgin olive oil
sea salt flakes and freshly ground
   black pepper
1 small clove garlic, peeled, halved
1 small ficelle baguette or 2 dinner
   rolls, sliced into 2 mm-thick ovals
50 g caster sugar, plus extra
   for sprinkling
25 ml hot water
50 g walnuts
⅓ cup soft fresh goat's curd
½ cup baby basil sprigs
nasturtium leaves (optional),
   to serve

Green Olive Tapenade
140 g pitted green olives
2 teaspoons salted capers, rinsed
2 white anchovy fillets
2 tablespoons extra virgin olive oil

1 For the green olive tapenade, place the olives, capers, anchovies and olive oil in a food processor and blend until smooth. Makes 125 ml. Leftover tapenade can be stored in an airtight container in the fridge for up to 7 days.

2 Bring a large saucepan of water to the boil with a good pinch of salt.

3 Preheat a fan-forced oven to 180°C.

4 Trim the asparagus by removing the woody ends (usually approximately 2 cm). Use the tip of a small knife to remove the little spurs up towards the head of the asparagus. Place a handful of ice in a bowl and cover with 250 ml water to refresh the asparagus, then set aside. Place the green and white asparagus in the pan of boiling salted water and cook for 2 minutes or until just tender. Carefully remove with a slotted spoon and transfer to the iced water. Leave to cool thoroughly, then remove from the ice water, drain and set aside on paper towel.

5 Mix the honey and mustard in a small bowl, then add the lemon zest and juice. Mix well and slowly whisk in 40 ml of the extra virgin olive oil, adding it one drop at a time. Add a pinch of salt and a twist of pepper and set aside.

6 Rub the garlic clove onto the sliced bread and place on a baking tray, then drizzle or brush with the remaining olive oil. Bake for 4–5 minutes or until light-golden brown. Remove from the oven and set aside.

7 Mix the sugar and hot water in a bowl to form a thick paste (slurry). Place the walnuts in the sugar mixture and stir to coat evenly, then drain. Place the drained walnuts on a baking tray lined with baking paper, then sprinkle with extra sugar. Bake for 10 minutes, stirring or moving around once or twice; they should become shiny and sugary. Remove from the oven and leave to cool.

8 Cut the asparagus into 4 cm lengths, reserving the tips, then toss with a little of the honey mustard vinaigrette.

9 To serve, spread the tapenade liberally onto a serving plate or dish and top with the asparagus. Spread the goat's curd on the toasted bread and arrange around the asparagus. Sprinkle with the candied walnuts and drizzle with a little of the vinaigrette. Toss the baby basil with a little vinaigrette and scatter carefully on top of the asparagus salad, then add nasturtium leaves, if using. Serve immediately.

Asparagus baked in salt crust with vinegar mayonnaise

Salt-crust baking is an age-old Mediterranean cooking method, often used for whole fish and meat. In this recipe (pictured over the page) the salt crust completely encases the asparagus, creating an oven-within-an-oven effect. The combination of salt imparted from the salt crust, vinegar from the mayonnaise and the simple flavour of asparagus is delicious. Make sure you don't let the asparagus sit in the crust for any length of time before baking because it will take on too much of the salt flavour. If the salt crust seems a bit too challenging you could simply roast the asparagus with olive oil, sea salt and thyme and serve it with the vinegar mayonnaise.

1   For vinegar mayonnaise, place shallot in a small saucepan. Add vinegar, thyme, garlic, bay leaf and sugar. Simmer over medium–high heat until it reduces to 2 tablespoons, approximately 15 minutes. Set aside to cool. Strain mixture, discarding solids. Transfer vinegar reduction to a bowl and add mustard and egg yolks. Whisk well. Slowly add olive oil, drop by drop at first and then in a thin, steady stream, until mixture emulsifies to form a mayonnaise. Makes 310 ml. Any leftovers can be stored in an airtight container in the fridge for up to 3 days.

2   For salt crust, combine salts and flour in a mixing bowl. Add egg whites and water and mix until a dough forms. Wrap dough in plastic film, then rest for 30 minutes in fridge. Roll out until 4 mm-thick.

3   Meanwhile, preheat a fan-forced oven to 200°C.

4   Cut dough into two 25 cm squares. Place half of the asparagus on one side of each piece of dough and roll dough around asparagus to form a rectangular parcel. Make sure there are no holes when sealing dough around asparagus. Trim edges.

5   Place asparagus parcels onto a baking tray lined with baking paper. Bake for 15 minutes. Remove from oven, then immediately cut around top of salt crust to create a lid.

6   Season with sea salt and serve with vinegar mayonnaise to the side.

SERVES 4 AS A SIDE DISH

225 g table salt
75 g rock salt
335 g plain flour
2 free-range egg whites
200 ml water
12 asparagus spears, woody ends
   trimmed and discarded
sea salt flakes

Vinegar mayonnaise
2 shallots, finely diced
200 ml champagne vinegar
1 sprig thyme
1 small clove garlic, sliced
1 fresh bay leaf
2 teaspoons caster sugar
2 teaspoons dijon mustard
3 free-range egg yolks,
   at room temperature
200 ml extra virgin olive oil

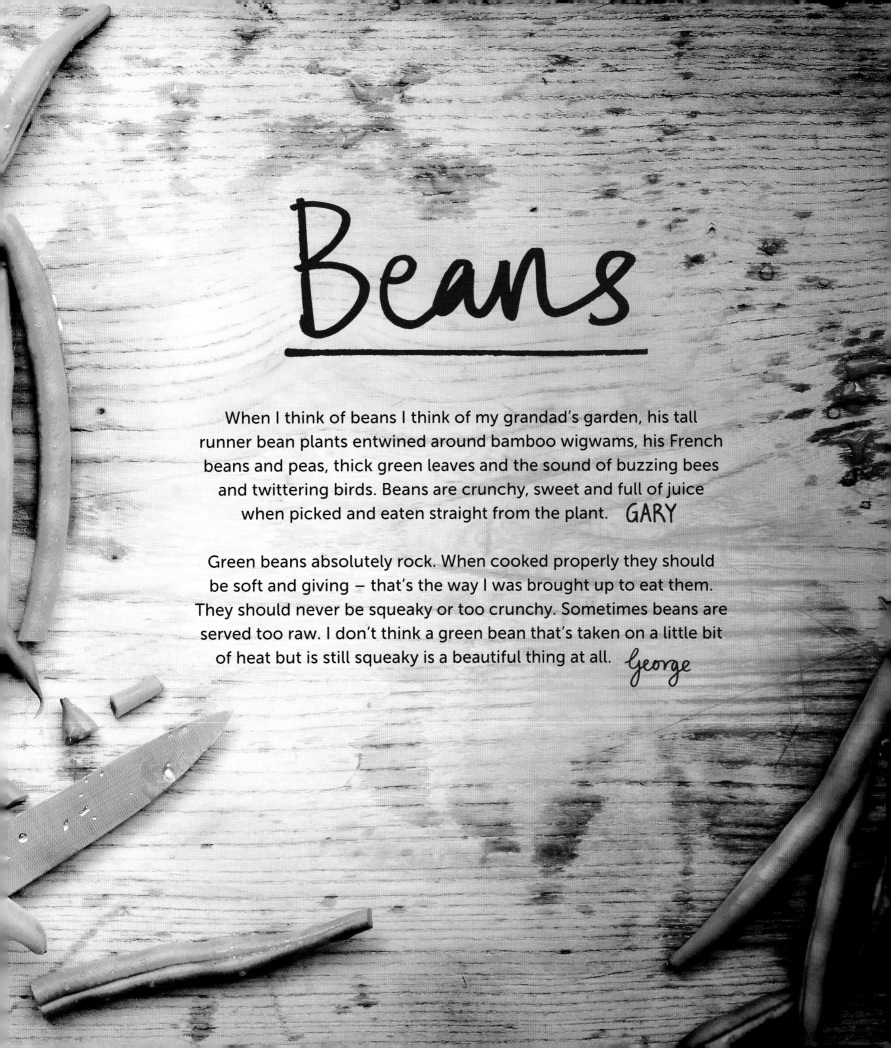

Beans

When I think of beans I think of my grandad's garden, his tall runner bean plants entwined around bamboo wigwams, his French beans and peas, thick green leaves and the sound of buzzing bees and twittering birds. Beans are crunchy, sweet and full of juice when picked and eaten straight from the plant. GARY

Green beans absolutely rock. When cooked properly they should be soft and giving – that's the way I was brought up to eat them. They should never be squeaky or too crunchy. Sometimes beans are served too raw. I don't think a green bean that's taken on a little bit of heat but is still squeaky is a beautiful thing at all. George

STIR-FRIED SNAKE BEANS AND GAI LAN

I am not a big fan of the pedestrian stir-fry, which always seems to contain baby corn, carrot and capsicum. But give me snake beans and gai lan, which are my favourite Asian greens, and it is a different story. To my mind, Chinese sausage and crisp garlic make everything taste great, so put them all together and you can't go wrong.

SERVES 4 AS A SIDE DISH

1½ tablespoons peanut oil
5 cloves garlic, finely chopped
1 handful snake beans, trimmed,
    cut into 8 cm lengths
1 bunch gai lan (Chinese broccoli),
    damaged outer leaves removed,
    stalks trimmed and thinly sliced
½ teaspoon chilli flakes
2 Chinese sausages (*lap cheong*,
    see page 266), thinly sliced
4 tinned water chestnuts,
    drained, sliced
2 tablespoons light soy sauce
2 tablespoons oyster sauce
1 large handful bean sprouts,
    straggly ends removed
1 small handful garlic chives
1 small handful coriander sprigs
steamed rice (optional), to serve

1   Heat the oil in a wok over medium heat, then add three-quarters of the garlic and, stir for 2 minutes or until golden and crisp. Drain the garlic into a sieve placed over a bowl, then place the garlic on paper towel to drain further and reserve the oil.

2   Wipe out the wok, return the oil to it and place over medium heat. Stir-fry the snake beans and gai lan gently for 3–4 minutes or until they begin to soften. Add the remaining garlic, chilli flakes and sausage to the wok, then increase the heat to high to crisp the sausage a little and release the flavour from the garlic. Add the water chestnuts, soy sauce and oyster sauce, then remove from the heat.

3   Tip onto a plate, then scatter with the bean sprouts, garlic chives, coriander and crisp garlic. Serve immediately, with rice, if desired.

Beans braised in olive oil and tomato

This is a delicious dish that tastes even better the day after you make it. My mum used to put this in my school lunch box, doused in olive oil, with some crusty bread on the side. Yum. You'll spend a whole day cooking this recipe but it's worth it. The most important thing is to cook the tomato sauce slowly to the right point and really extract the sweetness from the onions. The slow cooking infuses the beans with loads of flavour. However, if you like your beans firmer, just reduce the final roasting time.

1   Preheat a fan-forced oven to 120°C.

2   Place olive oil in an ovenproof saucepan over high heat. Add onion and garlic and sweat until translucent, approximately 5 minutes. Add tomato paste and 10 sprigs of the thyme and cook for 2 minutes, then add sherry vinegar. Add tomato and remaining thyme, then bring to a simmer. Place baking paper over tomato, then cover pan tightly with foil. Roast for 6 hours. Check and stir occasionally.

3   Increase oven temperature to 160°C. Place beans in a large roasting pan or baking dish and pour tomato sauce over beans. Sprinkle with coriander seeds. Place a sheet of baking paper directly over beans, then cover pan tightly with foil. Roast for 1 hour or until tender.

4   Serve warm or at room temperature.

SERVES 6 AS A SIDE DISH

300 ml extra virgin olive oil
3 onions, roughly chopped
2 cloves garlic, finely chopped
70 g tomato paste
14 sprigs thyme
50 ml sherry vinegar
1 kg tinned crushed tomatoes
500 g green or runner beans,
   tops trimmed
3 teaspoons coriander seeds

Beetroot

Beetroot has to have been the most 'in' vegetable over the past few years. Boiled and sliced, it has always been a salad favourite, but now it is a king of all things jellied, roasted, dried and foamed. I love the stuff! GARY

I love beetroot and cook with it a lot – raw, roasted, pickled, pureed, or shaved and doused in vinaigrette. Expect to get your hands dirty and stained a deep red. Even the green tops of the beetroot are delicious if you boil them for thirty seconds and douse them with olive oil and lemon juice. George

ROASTED BEETROOT SALAD WITH HAZELNUTS AND WATERCRESS

Beetroot and sour cream is a marriage made in heaven – just think of borscht, the ubiquitous Russian soup. Roasting beetroot is also the best way of bringing out that super-earthy sweetness you get from all root vegetables. This salad is a celebration of the earth and hedgerow; I have also added sweet roasted garlic, a few radishes and hazelnuts for interest and crunch, and watercress for its lovely, iron-y pepperiness.

SERVES 4 AS A LIGHT LUNCH OR SIDE DISH

1 red onion, quartered, root
   ends intact
sea salt flakes and freshly ground
   black pepper
4 sprigs thyme
8 cloves garlic
12 baby red beetroot, washed, stalks
   trimmed, bases scraped clean
12 baby yellow beetroot, washed,
   stalks trimmed, bases scraped
olive oil, for drizzling
50 g hazelnuts
100 g sour cream
4 radishes, cut into eighths
1 large handful watercress sprigs

Vinaigrette

1 teaspoon dijon mustard
2 tablespoons verjuice
   (see page 267)
1 tablespoon hazelnut oil
60 ml extra virgin olive oil
sea salt flakes

1   Preheat a fan-forced oven to 180°C.

2   Lay 2 large sheets of foil on the bench side-by-side. Place the onion on 1 sheet of foil, then sprinkle with a pinch of salt and a twist of pepper. Throw on 2 sprigs of the thyme and 4 of the garlic cloves.

3   Place the beetroot on the second sheet of foil, scatter with the remaining thyme and garlic, then season with salt and pepper. Drizzle the onion and beetroot with olive oil and enclose the foil around the vegetables to make 2 loose parcels. Transfer to a baking tray, then roast for 45 minutes or until tender. Remove the parcels from the oven and set aside to cool.

4   Peel the beetroot (preferably using disposable kitchen gloves otherwise you'll end up with stained fingers). Cut the red beetroot into quarters. Set aside.

5   Place the hazelnuts on a baking tray and roast in the oven for 4–6 minutes until the skins blister and begin to darken. Remove the hazelnuts and tip into a clean tea towel. Rub the hazelnuts with the towel to remove the skins.

6   For the vinaigrette, whisk the mustard and verjuice in a small bowl, then add the hazelnut and olive oils in a steady stream, whisking constantly to emulsify the vinaigrette. Season with a pinch of sea salt. Leftover vinaigrette can be stored in an airtight container in the fridge for up to 14 days and used to dress all kinds of salads.

7   Smear the sour cream onto a platter or individual plates, then top with the beetroot, onion and garlic. Sprinkle with the radish, hazelnuts and watercress, then drizzle with the vinaigrette. Serve immediately.

Beetroot and feta dip

I can't believe people would even think about buying readymade dips when you can make them so easily! The combination of beetroot and feta is like basil and tomatoes – a match made in heaven. Make sure the beetroot is cooked through or else it will be grainy when pureed. This dip is also great served alongside roasted scallops or fish, and char-grilled steak or lamb.

MAKES ABOUT 375 ML

500 g beetroot (about 1),
   tops removed
50 ml olive oil
5 sprigs thyme
1 teaspoon sea salt flakes
200 g feta, crumbled
toasted baguette or crusty bread,
   to serve

1 Preheat a fan-forced oven to 170°C.

2 Place beetroot in a deep baking dish. Splash with olive oil and scatter with thyme and salt. Cover tightly with foil and roast until a skewer passes through easily, approximately 1½ hours.

3 Wearing disposable kitchen gloves, peel beetroot, then place in a blender and blend until smooth. Wrap beetroot puree in a piece of muslin cloth and hang over a bowl (to collect any juices) in the fridge for at least 2 hours.

4 Process feta in a food processor until a smooth puree forms. Add beetroot puree and process until smooth and combined.

5 Serve with toasted baguette or crusty bread. Leftover beetroot and feta dip can be stored in an airtight container in the fridge for up to 3 days.

Berries

The appearance of soft berries on the greengrocers' shelves signals the arrival of summer. Ripe strawberries, loganberries, raspberries, blackberries and gooseberries offer a treasure trove of flavours. For me, blackberries will always evoke thoughts of England in late summer. There was once a railway track on Hayling Island that belonged to an old steam train called the Puffin' Billy. Old Billy has long since gone, and now the five-mile track is a thick row of oak trees, ferns and blackberry bushes. Through the snarl of thorns lie those little black jewels, which stain the lips and fingers of a delighted forager. GARY

Summer and berries go together. Sunshine plays such an important part in giving berries that flavour we love and they deserve. I don't have any favourites — they are all delicious. Use berries that are ripe and full of flavour. When you taste them you have to know they are worth eating. I love using berries in savoury dishes. Blackberries and wild mushrooms is an amazing combination. Or a simple wild mushroom fettuccine with some dehydrated blueberries thrown over the top. Delicious. George

SWEET-CHEESE CRUMBLE SOUFFLES WITH BLACKBERRIES

These sweet cheese souffles are opulent, extravagant and by far the lightest 'cheesecake' you will ever eat. The secret to achieving a perfect souffle lies in buttering the mould properly so it rises above the rim rather than catching on the sides. This is a simplified version of a crumble souffle I make in my restaurants, where I bake the souffle until the mixture has risen one centimetre above the rim of the mould and formed a skin, then sprinkle over the raw crumble mixture and continue to bake until the souffle has risen and is cooked perfectly. There will be extra crumble mixture leftover, which can be baked on top of your favourite fruit.

SERVES 4

25 g soft unsalted butter, plus
    extra for greasing
35 g plain flour
3 free-range eggs, separated
160 g caster sugar, plus extra
    for dusting
finely grated zest of 1 lemon
125 ml milk
125 g cream cheese
½ vanilla pod, split, seeds scraped
icing sugar, for dusting
Vanilla Ice Cream (see page 83),
    to serve

Crumble
50 g cold unsalted butter, chopped
75 g plain flour
50 g soft brown sugar

Blackberries
250 g blackberries
75 g caster sugar

1 Mix the butter and flour in a small bowl until a paste forms. Whisk the egg yolks with 40 g of the sugar in another bowl until pale and creamy, then add the lemon zest and set aside. Place the milk, cream cheese and vanilla seeds in a saucepan and whisk over low heat until the mixture is smooth and begins to boil. Whisking continuously, add tablespoonfuls of the butter mixture to the milk mixture until thick and smooth. Whisk for another 3 minutes, then remove from the heat. Whisk in the egg yolk mixture and combine well. Transfer to a bowl, cover closely with plastic film to avoid a skin forming, then set aside to cool.

2 For the blackberries, place the berries and the sugar in a small stainless-steel saucepan, then stand for 10 minutes. Simmer over low heat for 3–4 minutes; the berries should be soft but still hold their shape. Remove from the heat and set aside.

3 Grease four 250 ml-capacity souffle moulds well with extra soft butter, then refrigerate for 10 minutes. Grease again with butter lightly but evenly, then sprinkle each mould evenly with 1 tablespoon of the extra sugar and shake out the excess.

4 Preheat a fan-forced oven to 180°C.

5 For the crumble, rub the butter into the flour until the mixture resembles coarse breadcrumbs, then add the sugar. Spread the mixture over a baking tray and bake for 5 minutes or until light golden. Cool and set aside.

6 Using a whisk or hand-held electric beaters, whisk the egg whites with 60 g of the caster sugar until soft peaks form. Slowly add the remaining 60 g sugar and beat for another minute or until stiff and glossy. Using a large metal spoon, fold one-third of the egg white mixture into the souffle base to loosen it, then fold in the remaining egg white mixture.

7 Place 1 tablespoon of the blackberries in the base of each prepared souffle mould, then spoon one-quarter of the souffle mixture evenly on top. Place the moulds on a baking tray and bake for 12 minutes or until risen and golden.

8 Sprinkle the souffles with a little of the crumble mixture, dust with icing sugar and top with a spoonful of blackberries. Serve with the extra berries and ice cream to the side.

Strawberry and ouzo sorbet with buffalo yoghurt panna cotta

This dish is all about simplicity and elegance. The ouzo adds a lovely anise flavour to the strawberry sorbet and the buffalo yoghurt is super-creamy and offers a great balance to the sorbet. You'll need a candy thermometer to get the temperatures right. When we make this sorbet in the restaurant, we use twenty grams trimoline (an invert sugar available online or from specialty food stores) and sixty grams liquid glucose. As trimoline is difficult to source, I've adapted the recipe to make it more achievable at home, but this means that the sorbet won't be as creamy or last as long in the freezer.

1   Place strawberries and water in a small saucepan and simmer for 5 minutes. Transfer to a blender and blend until smooth. Return strawberry puree to pan and add glucose and sugar. Heat over medium heat until mixture registers 85°C on a candy thermometer. Remove from heat and add ouzo, then press with a spoon through a fine mesh sieve over a bowl. Cover with plastic film and refrigerate until cool. Transfer cooled strawberry mixture to an ice cream machine and churn following manufacturer's instructions.

2   For yoghurt panna cotta, heat milk, sugar and vanilla seeds and pod in a saucepan over low heat until sugar dissolves (60°C on a candy thermometer).

3   Meanwhile, place gelatine in a bowl of iced water until soft. Remove gelatine, then stir into milk mixture and leave until mixture cools (30°C on a candy thermometer). Whisk in yoghurt, then pour mixture into eight 125 ml-capacity dariole moulds or a large serving bowl. Refrigerate until set, approximately 3 hours.

4   Serve panna cotta with spoonfuls of strawberry and ouzo sorbet alongside and a sprig of dill to garnish, if desired.

SERVES 8

400 g strawberries, hulled, halved
600 ml water
120 g liquid glucose (see page 266)
480 g caster sugar
2 teaspoons ouzo, or to taste
dill sprigs (optional), to serve

Buffalo yoghurt panna cotta
250 ml milk
110 g caster sugar
1 vanilla pod, split, seeds scraped
5 leaves gold-strength gelatine
    (see page 266)
800 ml buffalo yoghurt
    (if unavailable, use natural sheep's
    milk yoghurt)

Cauliflower

This vegetable has been much maligned.
Bad memories of boiled mushy and sulphurous cauliflower
haunt us all. But treated well, cauliflower is one of my absolute
favourites. It's smooth as silk in a puree or soup and, when
roasted, it becomes sweet and slightly nutty.   GARY

Cauliflower is the only vegetable that I can say I use all year
round. It's not only great roasted, steamed or fried, but you can
even shave it and serve it raw or make it into one of the best
purees ever. For me, it's up there with potatoes in the
pantheon of versatile vegetables.   George

ROASTED CAULIFLOWER WITH CAULIFLOWER PUREE AND CONFIT OF FENNEL AND OLIVES

There is nothing better than applying different techniques to the same ingredient to make the one dish. By doing this you bring out a range of its characteristics, such as hot, cold, sweet, sour, smokiness, crunch, crispness or creaminess. Here, I've done this with a cauliflower, roasting some of it and pureeing the rest. How lovely an ingredient is when served in several ways; bang all those textures and flavours together and hey presto — what a dish.

SERVES 4 AS A LIGHT LUNCH OR SIDE DISH

1 head cauliflower, trimmed
200 ml milk
sea salt flakes
finely grated zest and juice of
    1 lemon
90 ml extra virgin olive oil, plus
    extra for drizzling
8 cloves garlic
3 sprigs thyme, plus extra for
    scattering
1 teaspoon sunflower seeds
1 bulb baby fennel, trimmed, cut
    into 5 mm dice, fronds reserved
1 star anise
90 g small black olives, such
    as nicoise or ligurian
crusty bread, to serve

1 Preheat a fan-forced oven to 180°C.

2 Cut off one edge of the cauliflower to give you a straight side. Cut 4 × 2 cm-thick slices across the width of the cauliflower and set aside. Shred the remainder finely (including the stalk) and place in a small heavy-based saucepan. Add the milk, a pinch of salt and lemon zest. Bring to the boil over medium heat, then simmer for 6–8 minutes or until the cauliflower is very tender. Drain and discard the milk. Blend the cauliflower in a blender until smooth and creamy. Set aside. Drizzle with olive oil.

3 Meanwhile, place a sheet of foil and a sheet of baking paper in a heavy-based roasting pan or ovenproof frying pan. Drizzle with 2 tablespoons of the olive oil and add the sliced cauliflower. Drizzle with 1 teaspoon of the olive oil and season with salt. Add the thyme and garlic and roast for 10 minutes. Turn the cauliflower slices over, scatter with sunflower seeds, then return to the oven for another 10 minutes until tender and golden on both sides. While the idea is to keep the cauliflower slices intact, don't worry if they break a little; it still looks (and tastes) gorgeous.

4 Meanwhile, place the fennel in a small saucepan. Pour over the remaining olive oil, then add 2 teaspoons salt, the star anise and a few fennel fronds. Cook the fennel over very low heat for 10–15 minutes or until it is nice and tender. Remove from the heat, then add the olives and 1 tablespoon torn fennel fronds. Add a squeeze of lemon and adjust the seasoning if required.

5 To serve, generously smear the puree over 4 plates and top with one-quarter of the warm cauliflower. Scatter with the fennel and olive mixture and sunflower seeds. The puree is delicious mopped up with a good-quality crusty bread.

'Maha' fried cauliflower

I stole this dish from my business partner Shane Delia, from Maha Restaurant in Melbourne, and I absolutely love it. Make sure you eat it hot as it goes soggy when it cools. It's as good as hot chips but marginally healthier. Serve this as a starter, side dish or mezze.

SERVES 4–6 AS A STARTER OR SIDE DISH

750 ml olive oil, for deep-frying
1 head cauliflower, trimmed, cut into florets (about 850 g)
½ teaspoon ground cumin
¼ teaspoon cayenne pepper
sea salt flakes

Walnut dip
100 g walnuts
1 heaped tablespoon tahini
juice of 1 lemon
2 slices white bread, crusts removed, soaked in water
100 ml cold water
100 ml extra virgin olive oil, plus extra for drizzling
sea salt flakes

1 For walnut dip, preheat a fan-forced oven to 160°C. Roast walnuts on a baking tray until lightly toasted, approximately 7 minutes. Place walnuts, tahini and lemon juice in a food processor. Squeeze bread of excess water, then add to food processor and blend well. With motor running, slowly add cold water and then olive oil until mixture emulsifies. Season with sea salt. Makes 375 ml. Any leftover dip can be stored in an airtight container in the fridge for up to 10 days.

2 Heat olive oil in a deep heavy-based saucepan until it registers 190°C on a candy thermometer. Working in small batches, deep-fry cauliflower until tender and golden, approximately 2 minutes; make sure oil returns to 190°C before adding next batch of cauliflower to pan. Remove with a slotted spoon and place on paper towel to drain. Season with cumin, cayenne pepper and sea salt.

3 Serve cauliflower immediately with a bowl of walnut dip drizzled with olive oil to the side.

Eggplant

Plump and deep purple, almost black, shiny skinned
eggplants are like little tom toms when you tap them with your
fingers. Botanically eggplants are classified as a berry. Their sponge-
like, seedy centres are bitter when raw but are totally transformed
by cooking, when their silky, delicate flesh takes on other
flavours so effortlessly and brilliantly. GARY

I love eggplant. But it's one of those ingredients that, if you don't
cook it properly, can taste awful – bitter, chewy and squeaky. Look
for the small baby Lebanese eggplants that aren't bitter; they are
very easy to cook. Work your way up to other dishes. If you're using
a large eggplant you'll need to salt it well to remove the bitterness,
then wash and dry it thoroughly before cooking it. George

EGGPLANT WITH BROWN-RICE MISO AND BONITO

I am a big fan of eggplant in all sorts of guises. Here I have used it with brown-rice miso and bonito to make one of my favourite Japanese dishes. The sweet and savoury flavours of the miso and bonito flakes are delicious and the smoky, yet silky eggplant hits the spot. Edamame is the Japanese name for soy beans. They are available frozen in pods or podded, in the freezer section of Asian food stores.

1   Mix the miso and sugar in a small saucepan. Add the mirin a little at a time. Stir over low heat for 10 minutes or until the mixture thickens and forms a paste, taking care not to catch the miso on the base of the pan. Remove from the heat and set aside.

2   Transfer 2 tablespoons of the miso mixture to a bowl. Add the boiling water to the bowl, then add the dashi powder, sesame oil and sake. Set aside.

3   Add a good pinch of salt and the edamame to a saucepan of boiling water and boil for 2 minutes, then drain. Set aside for 2 minutes to cool slightly. Pop the soy beans from the pods and discard the pods. Season the beans with a little salt and set aside.

4   Cut a thin slice from the top and underside of each eggplant so they sit flat on the bench, then score in a crisscross pattern on the diagonal about 1 cm into the eggplant. Heat the oil in a large heavy-based saucepan to 180°C, then carefully lower the eggplants into the pan and cook for 5 minutes. Reduce the heat slightly to low–medium and turn the eggplants over. Cook for a further 5 minutes or until tender. Drain well on paper towel, then spread with the miso and mirin paste.

5   Divide the eggplants among 4 shallow bowls, then scatter with the edamame, pour a little of the dashi broth around, sprinkle some bonito flakes over the top and serve.

SERVES 4 AS A LIGHT MEAL OR SIDE DISH

---

125 ml organic brown rice miso (see page 267)
2 tablespoons caster sugar
125 ml mirin (see page 267)
125 ml boiling water
1 × 7 g sachet dashi powder (see page 266)
1 teaspoon sesame oil
2 tablespoons sake
table salt
150 g frozen edamame (soy bean) pods
4 small eggplants
200 ml vegetable oil
2 tablespoons bonito flakes (see page 266)

Braised eggplant 'briam' with saffron yoghurt

What I love about Greek cuisine is its regionalism. Traditionally featuring roasted vegetables, this dish originated on the Greek island of Crete and is a staple lunchtime snack served with a glass of crisp wine. You could use any type of vegetable – generally vegetables that are on their way out are used up in this robust dish. I like using eggplant for its slippery and meaty texture. Store this in a jar in the fridge for up to three days, so you can help yourself to a spoonful whenever you like. It's fabulous with barbecued chicken or steak.

SERVES 4–6 AS A SIDE DISH

2 teaspoons coriander seeds
2 teaspoons cumin seeds
160 ml extra virgin olive oil
2 red onions, thinly sliced
1 clove garlic, thinly sliced
1 × 400 g tin crushed tomato
1 tablespoon sherry vinegar
1 tablespoon tomato paste
2 litres olive oil, for deep-frying
2 eggplants, cut into 2 cm cubes
2 teaspoons sea salt flakes
10 coriander leaves
10 mint leaves

Saffron yoghurt
small pinch of saffron threads
50 ml milk
200 g natural Greek-style yoghurt

1 Preheat a fan-forced oven to 180°C.

2 Place coriander and cumin seeds on a baking tray and roast until fragrant, approximately 5 minutes. Crush with a mortar and pestle.

3 Heat 1 tablespoon of the extra virgin olive oil in a saucepan over high heat, then add onion, garlic, coriander seeds and cumin seeds and sweat until onion is translucent, approximately 4 minutes. Add tomato, sherry vinegar, tomato paste and remaining extra virgin olive oil and cook over low heat for 45 minutes.

4 Meanwhile, for saffron yoghurt, place saffron and milk in a small saucepan over low heat for 2 minutes. Set aside on a bench for 1 hour to infuse. Add saffron milk to yoghurt and mix well. Cover with plastic film and set aside in fridge.

5 Meanwhile, heat olive oil for deep-frying in a large heavy-based saucepan until it registers 180°C on a candy thermometer, then fry eggplant in 3 batches for 2–3 minutes or until just tender; make sure oil returns to 180°C before adding next batch of eggplant to pan. Drain on paper towel.

6 Take tomato mixture off heat and add eggplant. Season with sea salt and set aside to cool. Finely shred coriander and mint, then add to cooled eggplant mixture.

7 Serve eggplant with a bowl of saffron yoghurt to the side.

Fennel

When I first came to Australia fennel wasn't available to buy.
Nobody used it, except the Italians and Greeks who grew it in
their gardens. I used to see it sprouting wild along the sides of the
railway tracks. Now we can't get enough of it, whether sliced thinly
in salads, grilled or roasted. With soft, milky mozzarella and the
sharpness of the pickled onion in the Fennel and Grapefruit
Salad on page 126, it's perfect. GARY

My mum would serve fresh fennel bulbs chopped into
quarters on the table at home to refresh the palate between
courses. I still prefer raw to cooked fennel; it's so refreshing
and you feel like you're putting healthy nutrients into your
body. Fennel's also lovely cooked on a char-grill, which
gives it a great, smoky flavour. George

FENNEL AND GRAPEFRUIT SALAD

For this recipe (pictured over the page) I thought of the freshest things I could and threw them together. All the flavours work brilliantly. You can substitute the grapefruit for orange or blood orange or for something a little different such as pomelo, which looks like a football-sized grapefruit with a coarse, cellular citrus structure inside. I feel positively slim and healthy just thinking about it!

SERVES 4–6 AS A LIGHT LUNCH OR SIDE DISH

60 ml red-wine vinegar
½ small red onion, thinly sliced
1 pink grapefruit
2 bulbs fennel, trimmed, thinly sliced, fronds reserved
2 rounds buffalo mozzarella
⅓ cup flat-leaf parsley leaves
⅓ cup spearmint, torn
sea salt flakes and freshly ground black pepper
60 ml extra virgin olive oil
½ teaspoon chilli flakes

1 Bring the vinegar to the boil in a small saucepan, then pour over the onion. Leave to pickle for 15 minutes or until cold. Drain before using.

2 Remove the skin and pith from the grapefruit and squeeze the skin over a bowl to catch any juice, then set the juice aside. Segment the grapefruit, then cut into bite-sized pieces.

3 Place the fennel and grapefruit on a large plate, then tear the mozzarella over the top and scatter with the pickled onion, parsley, spearmint and fennel fronds. Season with a pinch of salt and pepper.

4 Mix the olive oil with the grapefruit juice, then add the chilli flakes and season with salt and pepper.

5 Drizzle the salad with the dressing, then serve immediately with the remaining dressing offered in a bowl or jug to the side.

Fennel mornay

This dish (pictured over the page) is so simple and makes a great winter warmer. It uses Greek kefalograviera, a hard, sheep's milk cheese similar to parmesan, which imparts a real saltiness to the dish. (If you can't find kefalograviera, substitute parmesan.) Serve with the Sunday roast and watch everyone devour it. This is a good way to get kids to eat fennel; they love that whole cheesy thing.

SERVES 6 AS A SIDE DISH

300 ml milk
3 sprigs thyme
½ clove garlic, crushed
¼ onion, sliced
30 g unsalted butter, chopped
30 g plain flour
20 g kefalograviera cheese
   (see page 267)
3 bulbs fennel, trimmed,
   cut into 8 wedges

1 Place milk, thyme, garlic and onion in a heavy-based saucepan and infuse over low heat for 30 minutes. Do not allow to simmer (mixture should register 70°C on a candy thermometer, if you have one).

2 Melt butter in a heavy-based saucepan over low heat, then add flour and cook for 2 minutes, stirring constantly with a wooden spoon. Slowly add hot milk, straining it through a fine mesh sieve into pan and whisking it into butter so no lumps form. Grate kefalograviera cheese into mornay sauce. Stir to melt.

3 Preheat a fan-forced oven to 170°C.

4 Meanwhile, steam fennel over a pan of simmering water until tender, approximately 8 minutes. Transfer fennel to a small baking dish. Pour over mornay sauce and bake until golden brown, approximately 20–25 minutes.

5 Serve immediately.

Figs

They say you should never slice a fig but rather tease and tear
it open to reveal its soft, sweet and seeded heart. Our neighbour
has a massive fig tree, half of which hangs over into our garden and,
with his blessing, we pick kilos of the gorgeous fruit every autumn.
George's ice cream wrapped in fig leaves (see page 135) makes
me think of that tree – perfect. GARY

My parents' fig tree has to be the most prized possession
in their back garden. I'm not especially interested in varieties –
I love them all. The fig is one of the most ancient of fruits; you can
tell they've been around for a long time. You've got to be able to
stand near a fig tree, tear the fruit off and know it's been kissed by
the sun. When chefs say they've created the perfect dish they're
talking bull – there is no such thing. However, the tree
that grows these figs is perfect. George

ROAST DUCK WITH FIGS AND POMEGRANATE

SERVES 4 AS A MAIN

4 pomegranates
2 tablespoons caster sugar
4 duck breast fillets, skin
    scored lightly
sea salt flakes
2 sprigs thyme
1 clove garlic, peeled
8 figs, halved
extra virgin olive oil, for brushing
tarragon sprigs (optional), to serve

Duck is a strongly flavoured bird and can be fatty if not treated with the utmost care. Cooked well, however, it transcends the ordinary. Marrying duck with pomegranate and figs in this recipe takes it all to another level. It's both sweet and savoury, and is just bursting with flavour.

1   Roll the pomegranates on the bench, pressing down with your hands to loosen the seeds inside. Cut the pomegranates in half, then break into smaller pieces so you can remove the seeds easily into a bowl with your fingertips. Reserve 4 tablespoons seeds and set aside. Place the remaining seeds in a potato ricer (this is the simplest and cleanest way to extract the juice) and squeeze the juice into a small bowl. If you don't have a ricer, rub the seeds through a sieve over a bowl to extract the juice (this is a messier option).

2   Place a small saucepan over medium heat, then sprinkle in the caster sugar; the sugar will begin to melt and turn a light amber colour. Stir and continue to cook the sugar for 3–4 minutes or until it becomes a reddish brown. Pour in the pomegranate juice; take care as the steam may rise quickly. Stir the juice, then bring to the boil, reduce the heat to low and simmer gently for 5 minutes or until the juice has reduced by two-thirds and become slightly syrupy and sweet. As a rule, you should have about 80 ml finished syrup.

3   Place a large non-stick frying pan over high heat and heat for 1–2 minutes. Season the skin-side of the duck breasts with a little salt and place skin-side down into the dry pan. Reduce the heat to medium and cook for 15 minutes or until the skin is crisp and the fat has rendered down. Add the thyme and garlic, then turn the duck breasts over, reduce the heat to low and cook for a further 5 minutes, basting the duck a few times with the pan juices. Remove from the pan and leave to rest for 3–4 minutes.

4   Meanwhile, heat a char-grill pan over high heat, then brush the cut side of the figs lightly with olive oil and place cut-side down in the pan. Cook for 2–3 minutes, then remove from the heat.

5   Slice the duck breasts into three. Divide the duck and figs among 4 plates. Add the pomegranate seeds to the syrup and spoon the sauce over and around the duck, then scatter with tarragon, if using, and serve immediately.

Fig ice cream with sherry muscatel syrup

What's nice about this recipe is that you can use soft and bruised figs – the riper the better – to make the ice cream, and their leaves to serve it in. Don't freeze the fig leaves, though, as they'll deteriorate in the freezer.

1 Heat milk, cream, cinnamon, vanilla pod and seeds in a saucepan over low heat until just warmed through; do not allow to simmer. Remove from heat and set aside for 10 minutes, then strain.

2 Whisk egg yolks and 100 g of the sugar together. Poor one-third of warm milk mixture into egg yolks. Whisk well. Transfer milk and egg mixture to pan with milk. Using a wooden spoon, keep stirring mixture over low heat until it coats back of the spoon, approximately 10 minutes. Place custard mixture in fridge and leave to cool.

3 Place figs, remaining sugar, sherry vinegar and lemon zest in a small saucepan and bring to a simmer. Reduce heat to low and cook, stirring occasionally, for 45 minutes or until thick and jammy. Transfer to a blender and blend until smooth. Set aside to cool.

4 Add cooled fig puree to custard mixture. Transfer mixture to an ice cream machine and churn following manufacturer's instructions.

5 Meanwhile, for sherry muscatel syrup, place sugar, vinegar and sherry in a saucepan over low heat, then stir until sugar dissolves. Add muscatels. Cook syrup for a further 18 minutes over low heat; do not allow to boil. Remove from heat and set aside to cool.

6 Serve ice cream with sherry muscatel syrup to the side. For a special effect, wrap servings of ice cream in fig leaves and tie with raffia – each diner then unwraps the parcel at the table (see opposite).

MAKES 1.5 LITRES

500 ml full-cream milk
500 ml pouring cream
½ stick cinnamon
1 vanilla pod, split, seeds scraped
10 free-range egg yolks
140 g caster sugar
300 g purple figs (about 4),
    stems trimmed, quartered
1½ tablespoons sherry vinegar
finely grated zest of 2 lemons
fig leaves, washed (optional),
    to serve

Sherry muscatel syrup
80 g caster sugar
1 tablespoon sherry vinegar
250 ml cream sherry
150 g muscatels

Lemons

I couldn't live without lemons; they are a culinary necessity.
Everything in my kitchen gets a little sniff of lemon. I put it
in scones, fish mousse, homemade lemonade – even my
spaghetti and meatballs gets a little parsley, garlic and
lemon to add some zing. GARY

Last year I was fortunate enough to spend five days in Positano,
Italy. WOW, lemons are everywhere there and they are gorgeous.
My father always says Greek food without lemon is like
a woman without high heels. George

SUSSEX POND PUDDING

This is an interesting pudding that I'd read about for years but, until recently, had never got around to trying. I mean, how good can a few lemons encased in suet pastry really be? You find out when you cut into the pudding and the sweet, lemony contents spill out to create a lovely pool at the base of the pudding, hence the name. It is so simple that it seems impossible that it could taste so brilliant. How wrong I was – this pud is truly delicious and completely over-the-top. I have tried it with oranges and cumquats and it works equally well, so give it a go!

SERVES 4

225 g plain flour, plus 2 tablespoons extra for dusting

½ teaspoon table salt

1 teaspoon baking powder

110 g freshly minced suet (order from your butcher in advance, see page 267)

80 ml water

80 ml milk

200 g unsalted butter, chopped

200 g soft brown sugar

2 small thin-skinned lemons (such as meyer), quartered

1 vanilla pod, split

double cream or Vanilla Ice Cream (see page 83), to serve

1 Sift the flour, salt and baking powder into a mixing bowl and add the suet. Rub together with your hands to form a fine crumb (or process in a food processor). Add the water and milk and bring together with your hands to form a soft dough. Avoid over-kneading as this toughens the dough. (You may find that you need a tablespoon or two of extra water to make the dough soft and pliable.) Turn out onto a floured bench and roll into a ball. Wrap in plastic film and leave to rest on the bench for 10 minutes.

2 Use a little of the extra flour to dust the dough and roll it out into a 5 mm-thick round. Cut one-quarter of the dough out in the form of a wedge (similar to cutting a wedge of pizza from the whole) and set aside. Fold the larger piece of dough and use to line a pudding bowl (mine is 1 litre-capacity), overlapping the cut edges so the dough fits neatly into the bowl, leaving 2–3 cm overhanging.

3 Place 100 g of the butter and 100 g of the sugar in the pastry-lined bowl and press in the lemon and vanilla pod. Top with the remaining butter and sugar and press down gently; the filling should reach the top of the bowl.

4 To make the lid, roll the remaining pastry out so it is a little bigger than the diameter of the top of the bowl, then lay it on top of the butter and sugar. Brush the edge of the pastry with approximately 1 teaspoon water and enclose, using the overlapping pastry lid to seal in the filling. Cut a square of baking paper slightly larger than the size of the bowl, then place it on top of the pastry. Cover the bowl with a generous sheet of foil; make sure that you can press it down at least half-way down the outside of the pudding bowl. Secure the foil with kitchen string, tying it around the top of the pudding bowl so it will not fall off during cooking.

5 Place a saucer in the bottom of a saucepan with a tight-fitting lid large enough to accommodate the bowl; this protects the base of the pudding from direct heat. Place the bowl on the saucer, then pour in enough boiling water to come three-quarters of the way up its side. Pop on the lid and bring to the boil over medium heat. Reduce the heat to low and simmer gently for 4½ hours; topping up with boiling water if required. Turn off the heat and leave to stand for 10 minutes. Carefully remove the bowl from the pan. Remove the foil and paper from the top of the bowl and invert the pudding into a shallow serving bowl or plate.

6 Serve slices of pudding with a dollop of cream or vanilla ice cream.

Preserved lemons

Preserved lemons are a handy little thing to store in your pantry all year round. They bring a certain sweet saltiness to a huge variety of dishes. Use the rind to add a salty, sour note to salads and marinades for fish or meat destined for the grill, or toss thin strips or dice through couscous or rice. To sterilise the jars, wash thoroughly in hot, soapy water, then rinse well. Dry in a 100°C oven for ten minutes.

MAKES TWO 2 LITRE-CAPACITY JARS

20–24 lemons
sea salt flakes
3 sticks cinnamon, broken
    into pieces
6 star anise

1 Wash and scrub 10 of the lemons, then cut into quarters without cutting all the way through. Stuff each lemon with 1 tablespoon salt and some cinnamon. Squash into two 2 litre-capacity sterilised jars and close lids tightly.

2 Leave for 4–5 days in a cool, dark spot.

3 Juice remaining 10 lemons. Open jars and press down lemons, then add star anise and pour in juice, making sure lemons are completely covered; you may need to add more lemon juice.

4 Leave for at least 1 month in a cool, dark spot before using. Preserved lemons will keep for up to 3 months. After opening, store in the fridge.

Lettuce

Think of lettuce as one hundred different leaves that
make up the colour, flavour and texture of a summer garden.
When making salad, I also like to use soft border leaves like
nasturtium and perilla, edible flowers like chrysanthemum,
garlic and rosemary, and other herbs such as dill, sage and
tarragon – now that's a salad to fall in love with.   GARY

You need some relief with food sometimes, and relief comes in
the form of some simply dressed leaves or a beautiful crisp salad.
It's like taking a dip in the ocean. It can be something you have as
a main course, an entree or a side dish. I think of the lettuce family
as more than your typical iceberg or cos. I include cabbage, bitter
radicchio or witlof and different types of shoots; things that are
refreshing, crunchy and crisp but not too filling. George

SUMMER SALAD OF PEAS, BABY LETTUCE, FETA AND SPEARMINT

When I was growing up, a salad meant soft butterhead lettuce, cucumber and tomatoes – nothing wrong with that, but have a look at this recipe. Celebrate all the different leaves, soft herbs and lettuces you can buy. Make a simple, slightly sweet dressing, and voila! Oh, and maybe serve it with a Campari and soda with a little ice and a dash of orange juice for a perfect summer starter.

1 Preheat a fan-forced oven to 160°C.

2 To make the vinaigrette, whisk the mustard, honey, lemon zest and juice in a bowl. Add a pinch of salt and pepper and whisk. Drizzle in the olive oil, whisking continuously until emulsified. Set aside.

3 If using fresh peas, place in a small pan of boiling salted water and simmer over high heat for 2 minutes or until just tender. Drain and refresh in iced water or under cold running water until the peas are cold. Drain well on paper towel and set aside. If using frozen peas, thaw and drain on paper towel.

4 Line a baking tray with baking paper and lay the pancetta on the tray. Cover with another piece of baking paper and lay another baking tray on top to keep the pancetta flat. Bake the pancetta for 10 minutes or until it is crisp and golden. Set aside to cool. Break the pancetta into bite-sized pieces.

5 Place the lettuce, flowers, herbs and nasturtium leaves (if using) in a bowl and toss together gently. Place half of the peas and feta in a wide-based bowl, then drizzle with a generous amount of the lemon vinaigrette and season with a little salt and pepper. Place half of the lettuce leaves and flowers on top and interweave with the crisp pancetta, then scatter with a few more peas, drizzle with dressing and repeat until all the leaves, flowers, peas, feta, pancetta and vinaigrette are used.

6 Serve immediately.

SERVES 4 AS A STARTER

120 g fresh or frozen peas
ice cubes
8 thin slices flat pancetta
1 baby cos lettuce, damaged outer
   leaves discarded, inner leaves
   washed and dried
1 small green oak lettuce, damaged
   outer leaves discarded, inner
   leaves washed and dried
1 large handful unsprayed edible
   flowers, such as marigold, violets,
   nasturtium, wattle, lavender,
   rosemary and garlic or mixed
   soft herbs such as dill, tarragon
   and perilla
½ cup spearmint leaves
1 small handful nasturtium
   leaves (optional)
120 g feta

Lemon vinaigrette
1 teaspoon dijon mustard
1 teaspoon honey
finely grated zest and juice
   of 1 lemon
sea salt flakes and freshly ground
   black pepper
125 ml extra virgin olive oil

Whitebait salad

When I eat this dish I feel really healthy. It is a tasty number but must be eaten immediately or it goes soggy. Don't panic if you can't get your hands on every variety of shoot. Take this recipe as a guide and use whichever shoots you can find. The dressing really makes this salad. If you're vegetarian, omit the whitebait and fish sauce and enjoy. But I reckon Gary loves it with the lot.

**SERVES 4 AS A STARTER
OR LIGHT MEAL**

100 g flaked almonds
1 small witlof, thinly sliced
¼ wombok (Chinese cabbage),
   thinly sliced
1 small handful alfalfa shoots
1 small handful mung bean shoots
1 small handful snow pea shoots
1 small handful onion shoots
1 small handful garlic shoots
1 small handful lentil shoots
1 small handful radish shoots
1 tablespoon nigella seeds
1 tablespoon pumpkin seeds
olive oil, for deep-frying
200 g Australian whitebait
1 tablespoon plain flour

Dressing
2 tablespoons honey (I use Attiki)
finely grated zest and juice of 1 lime
2 teaspoons fish sauce
1½ tablespoons water

1 Preheat a fan-forced oven to 160°C.

2 Place almonds on a baking tray and bake until golden brown, approximately 8 minutes. Set aside.

3 Mix witlof, wombok and shoots in a large bowl. Add cooled almonds, nigella seeds and pumpkin seeds.

4 For dressing, place honey and lime juice in a small bowl and mix well, then add fish sauce, lime zest and water. Taste and adjust with more fish sauce or lime juice if desired.

5 Spoon dressing over salad and mix well.

6 Heat olive oil in a large heavy-based saucepan until it registers 180°C on a candy thermometer. Lightly dust whitebait with flour, then deep-fry for 2 minutes or until crisp. Remove whitebait and drain on paper towel.

7 Add whitebait to salad, mix lightly and serve.

Mushrooms

If I miss anything from Britain and Europe it is the availability
of wild mushrooms. Chanterelles and porcini are my favourites.
We have a few varieties here in Australia that are available in
autumn and winter, such as slippery jacks or pine mushrooms, and
Australian-grown truffles are starting to come onto the market. The
heady smell of truffles is truly exciting. Right now I am salivating
over the thought of little boudin blanc (see page 188) with beautiful
little exotic mushrooms . . . heaven! GARY

Mushrooms are earthy. Though farmed mushrooms are available
year round, the wild ones give us a real sense that the colder
months are on their way. What's amazing about mushrooms is that
they all have different textures and flavours – squeaky, crispy, soft,
meaty – and they are so versatile and good for you. George

PIZZA WITH GARLIC MUSHROOMS AND TALEGGIO

I've made a classic thin-crust pizza with my all-time favourite washed-rind soft cheese – taleggio. I love the soft oozyness it develops as it matures. Garlic mushrooms are also irresistible, so throw them together and wow, what a combination! All I can say is trust George to call his scallop dish (see page 152) a pizza when quite clearly it's not – clever, though, and it tastes fantastic…

1 For the pizza dough, put the flour, salt, sugar and gluten (if using) in a large bowl and form a well in the centre. In a small bowl, dissolve the yeast with 150 ml of the water and pour into the well. Add the remaining water and the milk to the mixture. Mix all the ingredients together to form a dough. Turn the dough out onto a floured bench and knead for 8 minutes or until smooth. Once the dough is quite smooth, work in the extra virgin olive oil until it is incorporated. Set the dough aside in an oiled bowl in a warm area, covered with a tea towel, for 1 hour or until the dough has doubled in size.

2 Remove the dough from the bowl and punch it to knock out the air. Divide the dough into quarters (about 180 g each), then roll into balls. Cover with the tea towel and leave to prove again for another 30–45 minutes or until doubled in size.

3 Meanwhile, place a heavy-based non-stick frying pan over high heat. Add 1 tablespoon olive oil and the mushrooms, then brown for 4 minutes, taking care not to toss or turn them in this time. Turn and cook on the other side for another 4 minutes. Sprinkle with a little salt and a twist of pepper, then add the garlic and parsley and cook for a few seconds. Remove from the pan and set aside.

4 Place a pizza stone in a fan-forced oven and preheat to 220–240°C.

5 Stretch the dough pieces out on a floured bench and transfer them to a semolina-dusted chopping board. Roll out 4 thin discs of dough to form 26 cm rounds, then brush with the olive oil, leaving a 1 cm border. Working in batches if necessary, scatter with provolone, then place the pizzas on the pizza stone and bake for 3–4 minutes or until the pizzas begin to puff and become light golden around the edges.

6 Divide the mushrooms between the pizzas and scatter with the taleggio, then tear the pancetta over the top. Scatter with the sage leaves, then drizzle with a little extra virgin olive oil and return to the oven for 3 minutes or until the cheese begins to ooze and the pancetta softens. Serve with rocket scattered over the top.

MAKES 4

olive oil, for cooking
4 large field mushrooms, brushed clean, thickly sliced
sea salt flakes and freshly ground white pepper
1 clove garlic, thinly sliced
⅓ cup flat-leaf parsley, chopped
150 g provolone cheese, grated
200 g taleggio cheese, sliced
8 thin slices flat pancetta
16 sage leaves
wild rocket, to serve

Basic pizza dough

750 g strong plain flour (see page 266), plus extra for dusting
1 teaspoon table salt
15 g caster sugar
30 g gluten (optional, see page 266)
2 × 7 g sachets dried yeast
450 ml lukewarm water
50 ml milk
60 ml extra virgin olive oil, plus extra for drizzling
semolina, for dusting

Mushroom, scallop and hazelnut 'pizzas'

I am a big fan of Spring Bay scallops from Tasmania. I love them because they are allowed to grow in cold waters with lots of good nutrients. This dish is lots of fun to make and eat as it takes the concept of a pizza and turns it into a dish starring scallops in the shell. Eat the pizza crust like crusty bread. Note that scallops in the full shell can be difficult for home cooks to find. Ask your fishmonger to order them; alternatively, buy double the number of scallops in the half shell. You can use the leftover scallops in a freeform tart using the same pizza base recipe, baked off with some olive oil and sea salt. Sweat down some mushrooms, throw in the scallops at the last minute, and serve on the pizza base.

SERVES 4 AS A STARTER

12 Spring Bay scallops, in shells
2 tablespoons extra virgin olive oil
2 shallots, finely chopped
1 small clove garlic, finely chopped
75 g shimeji mushrooms, wiped,
    thinly sliced
75 g oyster mushrooms, wiped
    clean, thinly sliced
50 g king brown mushrooms
    (see page 267), wiped clean,
    thinly sliced
50 g swiss brown mushrooms,
    wiped clean, thinly sliced
20 g unsalted butter
2 teaspoons finely chopped chervil
2 teaspoons finely chopped thyme
2 teaspoons finely chopped
    flat-leaf parsley
25 g hazelnuts
sea salt flakes
1 free-range egg, lightly beaten
rock salt (optional), to serve

'Pizza' dough
450 g strong plain flour
    (see page 266)
30 g soft unsalted butter
3 teaspoons caster sugar
30 g fresh yeast
200 ml warm milk
2 free-range eggs, lightly beaten
1 teaspoon table salt

1   For pizza dough, using an electric mixer fitted with a dough hook, mix flour, butter and sugar for 3 minutes. Dissolve yeast in warm milk, then add to flour mixture with eggs and mix for 6 minutes. Add salt and mix for 5 minutes. Cover with plastic film and leave to rest in the fridge for 1 hour.

2   Meanwhile, open scallop shells and remove scallops. Clean shells and remove membrane from scallops, keeping roe intact. Return scallops to clean shells and set aside.

3   Heat olive oil in a heavy-based saucepan, then add shallot and garlic and sweat over medium heat for 2 minutes. Add mushrooms and cook until light golden and soft, 5–6 minutes. Add butter to mushrooms to finish. Drain mushrooms on paper towel, then transfer to a bowl. Add chervil, thyme and parsley to mushrooms.

4   Preheat a fan-forced oven to 160°C. Place hazelnuts on a baking tray and roast for 8–10 minutes. Wrap hazelnuts in a clean tea towel and rub to remove skins. Lightly crush hazelnuts with a mortar and pestle, then add to mushroom mixture and season with sea salt to taste.

5   Increase oven temperature to 190°C. Take pizza dough out of fridge. Place a spoonful of mushroom mixture over each scallop in the shell, then cover with top shells.

6   Divide dough into 12 even pieces. Working with one piece at a time and keeping the others covered while you work, roll out each piece into a 20 cm-long log. Wrap the dough around the outside edge of 1 scallop shell, pressing gently to seal well. Transfer to a baking tray lined with baking paper and brush dough with a little beaten egg. Repeat with remaining dough, scallops and egg.

7   Bake until dough is golden brown, approximately 7 minutes.

8   Serve scallop and mushroom 'pizzas' immediately – on a bed of rock salt, if desired.

Onions

Shallots and baby onions are staples in my kitchens. They are
sweet and add tremendous flavour to all sorts of dishes and sauces.
My dad used to tell me a story when I was a kid about a guy at his
work who would eat onions out of his garden as if they were apples.
I didn't believe him — how disgusting! Yet the texture of onions is so
crisp, they are jammed full of vitamin C, they have anti-inflammatory
properties, are good for your hair, fingernails and eyes, and are the
basis of nearly every good dish I know. So why not? What better
way to celebrate the humble onion than eating it raw. GARY

What would we do as chefs and cooks without the onion
family? Used in bases for stocks, sauces and soups, onions are the
workhorses of the kitchen. But you can also make the humble
onion the star player in a dish like my braised onion pie on
page 157. They add a real meatiness to certain dishes.
For me, caramelised onions are like a vegetarian
meat. Yum, yum. George

SWEET-AND-SOUR ONIONS

Onions are super-sweet when caramelised in this recipe (pictured over the page), and adding a little hit of vinegar makes them irresistible. They work perfectly as an accompaniment to offal such as calves' or lambs' liver and gamey meats such as venison or even kangaroo. I also like to serve them alongside grilled or roast chicken or meaty fish such as blue eye trevalla and monkfish.

SERVES 4 AS A SIDE DISH

1½ tablespoons olive oil
20 baby onions, peeled, root
   ends intact
sea salt flakes and freshly ground
   white pepper
60 g caster sugar
100 ml sweet aged red-wine vinegar
25 g unsalted butter
50 ml water
4 sprigs thyme, plus extra (optional),
   to serve
2 fresh bay leaves

1   Preheat a fan-forced oven to 180°C.

2   Place a shallow, heavy-based, ovenproof frying pan or enamelled cast-iron casserole over medium heat and add the olive oil and onions and cook, stirring occasionally, for 4–5 minutes or until golden brown all over. Season with 1 teaspoon sea salt and a little pepper. Remove the onions from the pan and set aside.

3   Wipe the pan clean and return it to medium heat. Add the sugar and melt for 4 minutes or until golden. Pour in the vinegar and stir once or twice until the sugar dissolves. Simmer for 10 minutes or until reduced by two-thirds. Add the butter and water, then bring to the boil. Add the onions, thyme and bay leaves to the pan and gently stir, coating the onions in the syrup.

4   Transfer the pan to the oven and roast for 20 minutes, stirring once during this time, or until the onions are tender and you can press the tip of a small knife into them with no resistance.

5   Scatter with extra thyme sprigs, if desired, and serve.

Braised onion pie

This dish (pictured over the page) is a real ode to the allium family. It's my interpretation of the traditional spanakopita that Mum would make for us all the time when we were growing up. Instead of spinach, I've made the onions the heroes of the pie. The combined flavours of onion, shallots and leek are delicious with the ricotta and feta.

1 Heat olive oil in a heavy-based saucepan over medium heat and add onion, garlic, shallot and leek, then stir for 5 minutes. Add thyme and bay leaves, then reduce heat to low and cook until caramelised, stirring frequently to prevent onions from catching, approximately 45 minutes. Remove from heat and set aside to cool.

2 Discard bay leaves and thyme sprigs. Add ricotta and feta cheese to onion mixture and mix well.

3 Preheat a fan-forced oven to 170°C.

4 Spray base of a large roasting pan (mine is 30 cm × 24 cm) with olive oil spray, then line base and sides with baking paper. Brush 1 sheet of filo pastry with clarified butter. Place in base of pan, trimming to fit. Repeat with 7 more sheets of filo so there are 8 layers of pastry.

5 Place half of the onion mixture evenly over filo. Place another 3 buttered sheets of filo pastry over onion mixture, trim to fit, then brush with clarified butter. Place remaining onion mixture evenly over filo. Place another 7 buttered sheets of filo pastry on top and trim to fit again. Brush top layer with clarified butter, then sprinkle with salt. Bake until golden brown, approximately 45 minutes.

6 Serve warm. If you wish to make this pie in advance it can be reheated in a 180°C (fan-forced) oven for 15 minutes.

SERVES 6 AS A MAIN

150 ml extra virgin olive oil
12 onions, thinly sliced
4 cloves garlic, thinly sliced
8 shallots, thinly sliced
3 leeks, white part only, thinly sliced
10 sprigs thyme
2 fresh bay leaves
400 g firm ricotta cheese
400 g feta, crumbled
olive oil spray, for greasing
18 sheets filo pastry
200 ml clarified butter
    (see page 266)
sea salt flakes

Potatoes

Our big food retailers are only just beginning to realise that we want more from our spuds than all-purpose potatoes. Potatoes that fry, roast, boil and mash are not all cast from the same die. We can now buy potato varieties including sebago, kipfler, spunte, bintje, desiree, purple congo, nicola, king edward, toolangi delight, pink fir apple and russet burbank. All we have to do is learn how to use them! GARY

Potatoes would have to be one of the most versatile ingredients around. Mashed, made into chips, boiled or crushed – the list goes on. It is important to pick the correct potato for the job. You'd never use a chat potato for french fries, for example – you'd use a sebago instead. For mash, I'd use a floury potato like a sebago or desiree. As a cook, an important thing to understand is that if you end up with a bad potato dish, you've either picked the wrong potato or they were too 'sugary', which indicates they are old. At my restaurants, I get the chefs to test one potato from each batch delivered to make sure they're not too 'sugary', but a good greengrocer should be able to tell you. George

BAKED WEDGES WITH FENNEL AND CUMIN SALT AND HERB MAYO

I love George's recipe for egg and chips (see page 164) – it's soooo English and I wish I'd thought of it first. To tell you the truth, I am not surprised by his recipe. Whenever we have been out for breakfast together he loves boiled eggs with little toast soldiers that he can dunk into the yolk. One type of potato does not fit all purposes. I find that starchy, fluffy potatoes with a low sugar content, such as sebagoes and colibans, are best for roasting and frying. I recommend buying new season potatoes for best results, as the sugar content of spuds increases the longer they sit on supermarket shelves.

1 Preheat a fan-forced oven to 185°C.

2 Crush the cumin and fennel seeds with a mortar and pestle, then add the sesame seeds, a good pinch of pepper and olive oil. Place the potato wedges in a bowl and toss with the oil and spice mix.

3 Place the potato wedges and garlic in a roasting pan lined with baking paper and then sprinkle over the black sea salt. Bake for 30–40 minutes or until crisp and golden. Turn occasionally, if required.

4 Meanwhile, for the mayonnaise, place the eggs, mustard, vinegar and salt in a blender or food processor, then blend until creamy. Add 300 ml of the oil and blend until creamy. Add the remaining oil and blend until creamy. Add a squeeze of lime juice. Transfer to a bowl, then stir in the herbs. Cover closely with plastic film and store in the fridge until required or for up to 5 days. Makes 660 ml. You can halve the mayo recipe if you prefer.

5 Serve the crisp wedges and garlic (squeezed out of the skin) with the mayo.

SERVES 4

---

2 teaspoons cumin seeds
2 teaspoons fennel seeds
2 tablespoons sesame seeds
freshly ground white pepper
1½ tablespoons olive oil
4 potatoes, cut into
   wedges lengthways
10 large cloves garlic or elephant
   garlic (also called russian garlic)
2 teaspoons flaked black sea salt,
   (see page 267)

Herb mayo
2 × 55 g free-range eggs,
   at room temperature
2 tablespoons dijon mustard
1 tablespoon white balsamic vinegar
1 teaspoon sea salt flakes
600 ml olive oil
squeeze of lime juice
⅓ cup roughly chopped
   flat-leaf parsley
⅓ cup roughly chopped dill

My mum's egg and chips

This dish reminds me of coming home from school and Mum cooking me a quick snack of egg and chips. Russet burbanks are great for chips but if you can't find them try sebago or pontiac potatoes instead.

SERVES 2 AS A SNACK

800 g russet burbank potatoes, washed, dried well, cut into 2 cm-thick chips

table salt

2 litres extra virgin olive oil, for deep-frying

2 free-range eggs

2 pinches dried oregano

1 Place potato in a saucepan of salted cold water over high heat and bring to the simmer, then simmer for 4 minutes; potato should be tender but hold its shape.

2 Drain potato, then place in one layer on a paper towel-lined baking tray and leave in the fridge for 1–2 hours.

3 Heat olive oil in a large heavy-based saucepan until it registers 190°C on a candy thermometer. Fry chips in 2 batches until golden and crisp, approximately 6–8 minutes.

4 Place eggs in a small saucepan of boiling water and cook for 4–6 minutes.

5 Transfer chips to a mixing bowl and season with salt and oregano.

6 Crack tops off eggs and serve with chips.

Stone Fruit

I love stone fruit and relish their appearance at the start of summer.
It is impossible not to create delicious desserts with ripe nectarines,
apricots and peaches that are already beautiful. Cherries are extra-
special because their season is so short. I have to use them in
everything when they are at their best. GARY

When stone fruit are in full swing and have been smiled
upon by the sun, their luscious flavour makes it so much easier
for us cooks. Simply grill to bring out their sweetness – what more
do you want? Maybe some clotted cream for Gary... George

CHOCOLATE AND CHERRY CAKE WITH CREME DE CASSIS SYRUP

For me, cherries, like figs, are a sexy fruit, epitomised in a scene from the 1960s movie *Cleopatra,* where a young Elizabeth Taylor stains her lips red with a cherry! Their deep purple colour, sweetness and intense flavour work perfectly with bitter dark chocolate: a classic combination. The poached cherries for this cake are best made at least a day in advance to allow their flavours to develop. They will keep in an airtight container in the fridge for up to one month, or bottled in a sterilised jar and kept in a cool, airy cupboard, they will last for up to three months.

SERVES 8

150 g cherries, pitted
50 g caster sugar
2 tablespoons water
1 star anise
finely grated zest of ½ orange
2 tablespoons creme de cassis
100 g unsalted butter, chopped, plus extra for greasing
60 g plain flour
60 g ground almonds
125 g icing sugar, plus extra for dusting (optional)
4 free-range egg whites (from 55 g eggs)
100 g dark couverture chocolate buttons (70 per cent cocoa solids, see page 266)

1   Place the cherries in a small saucepan and sprinkle with the sugar and water. Add the star anise and orange zest and leave to stand for 10 minutes. Pour in the creme de cassis and bring quickly to the boil over high heat. Leave to cool. Transfer the mixture to an airtight container, then refrigerate, preferably for 24 hours.

2   Preheat a fan-forced oven to 180°C.

3   Grease and line a 25 cm × 18 cm lamington tin with baking paper.

4   Melt the butter in a small saucepan over low heat until it bubbles and just becomes nut-brown. Remove from the heat and leave to cool for 5 minutes.

5   Sift the flour, ground almonds and icing sugar into a mixing bowl and set aside.

6   Place the egg whites in a mixing bowl and beat lightly with a fork. Mix in the flour mixture until combined. Stir in the melted butter and add the chocolate, then leave to stand for 10 minutes.

7   Spoon the mixture into the lamington tin. Drain the cherries, reserving the syrup, then gently press them onto the surface of the batter in rows. Bake the cake for 20 minutes or until it has risen and is slightly firm to the touch. Remove from the oven and leave to cool slightly before removing from the tin.

8   Leave the cake to cool completely, then slice. Dust with icing sugar (if using). Serve with the creme de cassis syrup.

Caramelised apricots with rosewater syrup

My mum uses rosewater a lot in her cooking. Warm apricots (you could even barbecue them) doused with rosewater syrup are just delicious. Keep the leftover syrup in a sealed jar in the fridge. It's gorgeous spooned over a simple panna cotta such as the one on page 111, or make your own baklava and drizzle the syrup over the top after baking. You can also poach fruit in it or pour it over ice cream.

SERVES 4

100 g soft brown sugar
4 large apricots, halved, stoned
1 tablespoon sherry vinegar
50 ml orange juice
slivered pistachios, to serve
micro herbs (optional,
   see page 267), to serve

Rosewater syrup
200 ml water
200 g white sugar
1 tablespoon rosewater

1   For rosewater syrup, combine water, sugar and rosewater in a saucepan and bring to the boil over low heat, stirring until sugar dissolves. Simmer until reduced and syrupy, approximately 4–5 minutes. Remove from heat and set aside. Any leftover syrup will keep in an airtight container in the fridge for up to 1 month.

2   Place sugar in a heavy-based frying pan over high heat until just melted and caramelised, taking care not to let it burn, approximately 5 minutes.

3   Place apricots in caramelised sugar, cut-side down, and cook for 3–4 minutes or until well-coated in caramel. Add sherry vinegar and orange juice and continue to cook for 1 minute, tossing gently to coat.

4   Serve apricots on plates or shallow bowls, drizzled with a little rosewater syrup and scattered with pistachios and micro herbs, if using.

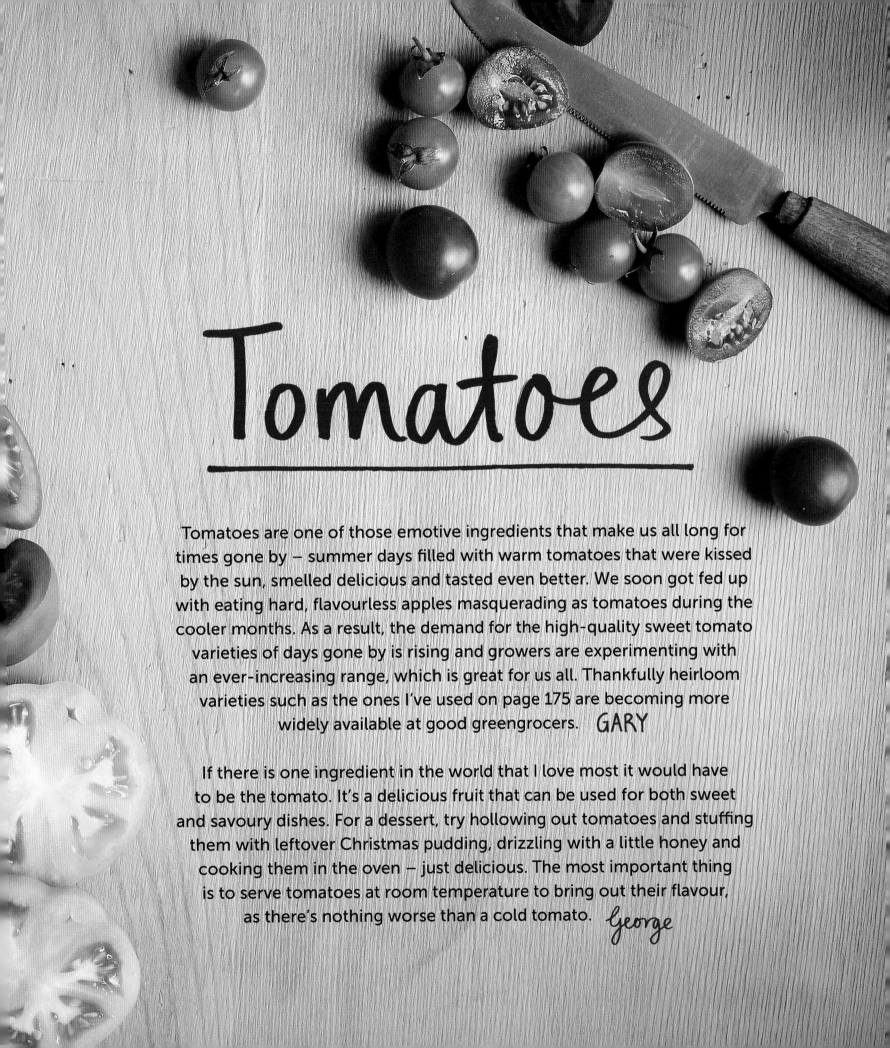

Tomatoes

Tomatoes are one of those emotive ingredients that make us all long for times gone by – summer days filled with warm tomatoes that were kissed by the sun, smelled delicious and tasted even better. We soon got fed up with eating hard, flavourless apples masquerading as tomatoes during the cooler months. As a result, the demand for the high-quality sweet tomato varieties of days gone by is rising and growers are experimenting with an ever-increasing range, which is great for us all. Thankfully heirloom varieties such as the ones I've used on page 175 are becoming more widely available at good greengrocers. GARY

If there is one ingredient in the world that I love most it would have to be the tomato. It's a delicious fruit that can be used for both sweet and savoury dishes. For a dessert, try hollowing out tomatoes and stuffing them with leftover Christmas pudding, drizzling with a little honey and cooking them in the oven – just delicious. The most important thing is to serve tomatoes at room temperature to bring out their flavour, as there's nothing worse than a cold tomato. George

CONFIT OF TOMATOES

I learnt this recipe many years ago from someone who worked for the famous French chef Joël Robuchon. At the time I thought, 'What a lovely, simple way to treat such an emotive ingredient'. The coriander adds a subtle background flavour and spice to fresh ripe tomatoes. Served with grilled fish, chicken or roast lamb, these are gorgeous, or simpler still, just slice or crush onto grilled sourdough bread – mmm!

1 Preheat a fan-forced oven to 100°C.

2 Select a baking dish or roasting pan that is large enough to hold the tomatoes in one layer (mine is 50 cm × 30 cm × 24 cm). Lightly crush the peppercorns, fennel seeds and coriander seeds with a mortar and pestle, then sprinkle over the base of the pan. Scatter on the salt and garlic, then add the star anise and evenly spread the mixture over the base of the pan. Place the tomatoes cut-side down (if halved) on top of the spices. Roughly tear the basil sprigs over the tomatoes, then place the basil stalks in between the tomatoes and flood with the olive oil.

3 Roast the tomatoes for 1 hour. Remove from the oven and leave to cool, then cover and refrigerate. You can serve these straight away or store in the fridge for up to 1 week. The tomatoes will continue to absorb the beautiful flavours of the other ingredients during this time.

SERVES 4 AS A SIDE DISH

1 teaspoon white peppercorns
2 tablespoons fennel seeds
2 tablespoons coriander seeds
1 teaspoon sea salt flakes
3 cloves garlic, bruised
4 star anise
1 kg mixed heirloom tomatoes, such as black russians, yellow plum, vine-ripened (see page 267), halved widthways (optional)
1 handful of basil sprigs
400 ml extra virgin olive oil

Salad of tomato, watermelon and manouri

SERVES 4 AS A STARTER OR SIDE DISH

4 black russian tomatoes
  (see page 267)
16 cherry tomatoes, halved
8 yellow cherry tomatoes, halved
extra virgin olive oil, for drizzling
sea salt flakes
200 g watermelon, rind removed
  and discarded, cut into
  2 cm cubes
100 g manouri cheese
  (see page 267)
nasturtium leaves (optional),
  to serve

This dish is simplicity to the max. Its success relies on sourcing great ingredients and serving them simply. I love to use a mixture of tomatoes to showcase their different colours, sizes and flavours. Black russian tomatoes are an heirloom variety with a very dark red interior and purple-tinged skin. If you can't get manouri (a fresh Greek cheese similar to Italian stretched-curd cheeses), use bocconcini, burrata or firm ricotta instead. You can dress this dish up for a dinner party, with ingredients carefully plated up individually, or serve it as a more rustic salad on a shared platter.

1 Cut the tomatoes into nice, presentable, even-sized pieces. Place tomato in a large mixing bowl. Coat with olive oil and season with some sea salt. Make sure tomato is at room temperature before serving.

2 Place tomato and watermelon randomly on a platter or 4 small plates (here I've used a chopping board). Break manouri cheese apart and scatter over and around tomato and watermelon. Scatter with nasturtium leaves, if desired.

3 Serve immediately.

lu

O

Veal

Rabbit

ed Meat

BUTCHER

chicken

fal

Lamb

Beef

Beef

To be honest, it's hard to pick a cut of beef that I don't like.
The sweet or tender cuts such as rib and rump are my favourites,
but when it comes to a Chinese-style red braise (see page 182),
short ribs are the absolute best. They are thickly cut, packed full
of flavour and good value to boot.   GARY

When you eat beef it's got to taste like beef. We sometimes get
too carried away by how tender the beef is, when I think we really
need to think about how tasty it is. Occasionally you need to chew –
God gave us teeth, after all! Think beyond the premium cuts to
things like what the French call *onglet*, a beautiful cut with
a really livery flavour, while the cheeks are gorgeous braised
to a gelatinous softness. Everyone needs a beef hit
every now and again. *George*

RED-BRAISED BEEF AND DAIKON

The pleasure of this dish (pictured over the page) lies in the lovely stock, so make sure that there's plenty of it to go around – you may like to serve this as more of a steaming hot wet dish. Bean and chilli sauce or paste is made from fermented soy beans and chillies – it can be purchased from Asian food stores.

SERVES 4 AS A MAIN

20 g dried shiitake mushrooms,
  soaked in hot water for
  45 minutes
60 ml peanut oil
800 g short beef ribs, cut into
  sections between the bones
2 tablespoons bean and chilli sauce
5 cm knob ginger, sliced
10 cloves garlic, peeled
1 teaspoon Sichuan pepper
1 fresh long red chilli,
  finely chopped
100 g yellow rock sugar
  (see page 267)
2 litres chicken stock
125 ml light soy sauce
125 ml dark soy sauce
375 ml Chinese rice wine
3 pieces dried mandarin or
  tangerine peel
5 sticks cinnamon
8 star anise
1 daikon, cut into 3 cm-thick pieces
1 onion, cut into 8 wedges
8 spring onions, cut into
  2 cm lengths
1 teaspoon sesame oil
coriander leaves and steamed rice
  (optional), to serve

1 Drain the mushrooms, reserving the strained soaking liquid, then remove and discard the woody stalks.

2 Heat a heavy-based saucepan or enamelled cast-iron casserole over high heat and add the peanut oil. Add the beef in batches and cook until browned on all sides and nicely caramelised. Reduce the heat to low, then discard any excess oil. Return all the beef to the pan. Add the bean and chilli sauce and cook for 1 minute, then add the ginger, garlic, Sichuan pepper, chilli, rock sugar, stock, soy sauces, rice wine, citrus peel, cinnamon and star anise.

3 Bring to the boil over high heat, then reduce the heat to low. Add the mushrooms, reserved soaking liquid, daikon and onion, then pop on a lid and simmer for 2 hours or until the beef is soft and tender. Add the spring onion and sesame oil, then scatter with coriander and serve with steamed rice, if desired.

Beef carpaccio with flavours of a hamburger

I am not a big fan of eye fillet, but served super-fresh and as a carpaccio I love it. This dish (pictured over the page), with its various ingredients, is like a little journey as you eat it. It's about lots of freshness and super-yummy flavours; it's also low in fat and very healthy. You can be as creative as you like — these are the things I like in my burger, but it's up to you. I know Gary loves it.

1   Preheat a fan-forced oven to 170°C.

2   Place beetroot in a small baking dish, drizzle with 1 tablespoon of the olive oil and sprinkle with 1 teaspoon sea salt. Bake for 25 minutes or until tender. Remove from oven and, when cool enough to handle, peel. Toss with remaining olive oil and set aside to cool.

3   Cut beef into 8 thin slices, then place between 2 pieces of plastic film and press gently but firmly with a rolling pin until thin and even. Divide between 2 plates and scatter with tomato, cornichon, shallot and cooled beetroot. Place small quenelles (spoonfuls) of mustard beside the beef.

4   Bring a small saucepan filled three-quarters with water to the boil, then reduce heat to low. The water should be just moving. Meanwhile, line 2 small cups or bowls with plastic film, leaving 5 cm overhanging. Drizzle in a little extra virgin olive oil and carefully crack an egg into each, then season with a pinch of salt. Gather the overhanging plastic film up to enclose the egg, lift out of the cup, then gently press with your fingers to expel any air. Twist the plastic film to tighten and shape the eggs, then tie off with kitchen string. Place eggs carefully into simmering water and poach for 6 minutes. Remove with a slotted spoon and snip plastic film at knots, then carefully remove eggs.

5   Carefully place 1 egg on each plate, scatter with nasturtium and snow pea sprouts (if using) and sage leaves, drizzle with remaining extra virgin olive oil and serve.

SERVES 2 AS A STARTER

6 baby beetroot, tops trimmed
2 tablespoons olive oil
sea salt flakes
1 × 150 g piece centre-cut aged
    beef eye fillet
6 baby black russian tomatoes
    (see page 267), halved
6 cornichons (see page 266),
    halved lengthways
2 small shallots, thinly sliced
2 teaspoons wholegrain mustard
1 tablespoon extra virgin olive oil
2 very fresh free-range eggs
baby nasturtium and snow pea
    sprouts (optional) and sage leaves,
    to serve

chicken

My mum tells me that chicken used to be a treat.
It was expensive, which is hard to believe these days as chicken has
become a staple in most households. I only buy free-range eggs and
chicken, which I believe is ethically the right thing to do. It may
have taken Jamie Oliver and Hugh Fearnley-Whittingstall to hammer
the message home, but they have changed how we eat in my
house, and in thousands of homes just like ours.   GARY

Chicken is the most commonly eaten meat in Australia. Look past
the breast and legs to the wings, oysters, ribs, neck and bones.
Chicken bones are the basis for any good stock or sauce. I absolutely
love Gary's boudin blanc (see page 188) — these French-style
sausages are delicate, tasty and use the breast of the chicken,
so without wasting any of your chook you can use the legs
to make my dish (see page 191).   George

BOUDIN BLANC WITH MUSHROOMS

SERVES 4 AS A MAIN

2 slices white bread, crusts removed

70 ml milk

200 g chicken breast fillets,
   roughly chopped

table salt

3 free-range egg whites

150 ml thickened cream

finely grated zest of 1 lemon

100 g thin salted sheep's casings
   (about 1.5 m, order from your
   butcher), soaked

60 ml olive oil

50 g unsalted butter

400 g exotic mushrooms, including
   enoki, oyster, shimeji and king
   browns (see page 267), trimmed,
   large mushrooms thickly sliced

2 cloves garlic, crushed

2 small fresh bay leaves, plus extra
   (optional), to serve

sea salt flakes and freshly ground
   white pepper

squeeze of lemon juice

2 tablespoons chopped
   flat-leaf parsley

rosemary sprigs (optional), to serve

Boudin blanc translates from French to English as 'white sausage'. You will find examples of this type of sausage all over Europe, but none as smooth and sophisticated as this French version. They are soft, delicate and the use of bread in the mixture (known as a *panade*) serves to lighten their texture further as they cook. While you only need about 100 g of casings (salted intestines used in sausage making) for this recipe, they are difficult to purchase in such a small amount, so soak and wash what you need and store the remainder in salt in the fridge for up to eight weeks, ready for the next time you wish to make your own sausages.

1 Soak the bread in the milk and squeeze away any excess, then set aside.

2 Blend the chicken and a pinch of salt in a food processor until smooth, then add the egg whites and blend until the mixture becomes firm. On a low speed, slowly add the cream in a steady stream. Add the bread and lemon zest and blend for 30 seconds to combine. Transfer this chicken mousse to a bowl, then cover with plastic film and place in the fridge so as it stays cold.

3 Drain the sheep's casings and rinse under cold running water. Run clean water through the casings to make sure they are thoroughly clean.

4 Place the chicken mousse filling into a piping bag fitted with a 1.5 cm-wide nozzle. Place the open end of a piece of the sheep's casings over the nozzle, drawing enough casing over the nozzle to make 6 sausages that are 4–6 cm long (ensure that there is at least 36 cm length of the casing). Gently squeeze the end of the piping bag, holding a little tension on the tip of the nozzle and the casing so the mixture fills the sausage skin. Tie the casing at 4–6 cm intervals with kitchen string. Repeat the process with another 2 pieces of casing so you have 16 even-sized sausages. This is difficult so it is best to repeat the process until all the mousse is used.

5 Place the sausages in a saucepan, then cover with cold water and bring to a gentle simmer over low–medium heat. Once bubbles start to appear on the surface of the water, reduce the heat to low and cook for 5 minutes; the water should barely move. If the temperature gets too high, the sausages will burst. Turn off the heat and leave to stand for 10 minutes, then remove the sausages from the pan. Drain and pat dry with paper towel. When the sausages are quite cold, carefully peel off the casings and discard the skins.

6 Place a dash of olive oil in a non-stick or enamelled cast-iron frying pan over medium heat. Cook the sausages for 2–3 minutes, turning until light golden all over. Remove from the pan and set aside. Increase the heat to high and add another dash of olive oil and the butter. Add the mushrooms and cook for 1 minute, then add the garlic and bay leaves and cook for 3 minutes or until the mushrooms are golden brown all over. Season with a sprinkle of salt and a twist of pepper, then add the lemon juice and parsley. Return the sausages to the pan, moving them around gently to coat with the mushroom mixture. Serve, scattered with extra bay leaves and rosemary, if desired.

Braised chicken and celery fricassee

I use chicken maryland (leg and thigh) for this recipe as I think the brown meat has much more flavour and is juicier than the breast. It's very Greek to finish a dish with egg and lemon – and you know why? The flavours are great! My mum would often make a classic Greek soup using chicken broth thickened and enriched with egg and lemon.

1   Preheat a fan-forced oven to 160°C.

2   Heat olive oil in a heavy-based frying pan over medium heat and seal the chicken pieces, turning until golden brown on both sides, approximately 5 minutes. Transfer chicken to a flameproof roasting pan and season well with salt.

3   Sweat celery, onion, garlic and oregano in the frying pan over medium heat for 4–5 minutes. Place over chicken pieces, along with thyme. Pour over chicken stock. Cover tightly with foil and bake for 1¼–1½ hours or until chicken is tender.

4   Remove chicken pieces from roasting pan, then place pan over medium heat, bring liquid to the boil and reduce by half. Add lettuce, dill and lemon juice to reduced stock.

5   Whisk eggs in a bowl until light and foamy. Add 125 ml of the hot stock and whisk to combine well, then pour egg mixture into pan. Stir over low heat for 2–3 minutes or until mixture thickens slightly; do not boil as the mixture will curdle. Season to taste with salt.

6   Return chicken to pan to warm through, then serve immediately, scattered with herbs, if desired.

SERVES 4 AS A MAIN

60 ml olive oil
4 chicken marylands
sea salt flakes
6 sticks celery, thinly sliced
1 onion, diced
3 cloves garlic, finely chopped
2 teaspoons dried oregano
3 sprigs thyme
1.5 litres chicken stock
1 iceberg lettuce, trimmed, cut into 3 cm squares
½ cup chopped dill
100 ml lemon juice
4 free-range eggs
dill sprigs and garlic chive buds (optional), to serve

Cured Meat

To pick salted beef as my choice of cured meat might seem strange when I could have chosen a nice jamon or bresaola, which are far more mainstream these days, and much more 'now'. However, I love the combination of salted beef and cotechino in the Italian dish bollito misto (see page 194). The horseradish salsa in my accompanying recipe works well with pretty much anything.   GARY

Having a Cypriot mother I've had the opportunity to eat great and interesting cured meats all my life. Lounza is very typical of the cured meats from Cyprus. We cure all our own meats at Hellenic Republic, including making our own lounza, but you can get it fairly easily at good Middle Eastern delis.   George

BOLLITO MISTO WITH HORSERADISH SALSA VERDE AND HERB DUMPLINGS

Some people are uncomfortable cooking and eating tongue; however, it is a beautiful meat when braised in a bollito misto. If you are a bollito misto first-timer, it might be an idea to use one or two of the meats (such as chicken and brisket) as this is easier than juggling lots of different items when it comes time to serve. The brisket and ox tongue will need to be ordered from your butcher. Cotechino is a large, Italian sausage made from pork meat, fat and rind that originated in the city of Modena. It can be purchased from Italian butchers and good delis. You will need a very large stockpot (at least 12 litres) to make this.

1 Soak the beef and tongue together in a large bowl of fresh water for 2–3 hours, changing the water 2 or 3 times.

2 Drain the beef and tongue, then place in a large heavy-based stockpot (at least 12 litre-capacity) and cover with the water. Bring to the boil over high heat, skimming and discarding any foam and scum that rise to the surface. Cook for 1½ hours, topping up with water to keep the meat submerged.

3 Add the carrots, onions, fennel, thyme, rosemary, peppercorns, fennel seeds, celery and garlic. Add the chicken and cotechino sausage and simmer for a further 1 hour. Pierce the thigh of the chicken to see if the juices are clear. If so, turn off the heat and leave to stand for 10 minutes. You can test the tongue and brisket by pushing a roasting fork into the meat all the way through; if there is only a little resistance, they are done. Transfer the meat and vegetables to a large tray or plate and set aside in a warm place covered with plastic film.

4 For the herb dumplings, mix the suet, flour, a pinch of salt and herbs in a large bowl. Make a well in the centre, then pour in the water and mix gently by hand to form a soft, supple dough; a little extra flour may be needed. Form into 2 cm balls and drop into the pan of hot stock. Bring to the boil, then reduce to a simmer and cook for 6–8 minutes. Turn off the heat.

5 Meanwhile, for the horseradish salsa verde, soak the bread in the vinegar for 5 minutes. Squeeze out the excess liquid and place bread in a blender with the horseradish, garlic, chervil, tarragon and parsley. Add extra virgin olive oil, ½ teaspoon sea salt and a twist of pepper, then blend to a rough green paste. Store in an airtight jar with a little olive oil on top in the fridge for up to 3 days. Makes 250 ml.

6 Remove the skin from the tongue and trim the base of all uneven fatty meat. Slice the tongue, brisket and cotechino. Divide the chicken into eight pieces, removing the skin if you wish. Cut the vegetables into big chunks.

7 Divide the meat, vegetables and dumplings among bowls, then ladle in a little stock. Drizzle with extra virgin olive oil, top with a spoonful of horseradish salsa verde and serve. (Freeze any leftover dumplings in an airtight container to add to your next stew.)

SERVES 6–8 AS A MAIN

1 × 600 g piece salted brisket
1 × 900 g ox tongue
4 litres water
4 carrots, peeled
2 onions, peeled
1 bulb fennel, trimmed
10 sprigs thyme, tied in a bundle
1 stalk rosemary
1 teaspoon white peppercorns
1 teaspoon fennel seeds
6 sticks celery, washed, trimmed,
    quartered lengthways
6 cloves garlic, peeled
1 × 1 kg free-range chicken
1 cotechino sausage (about 700 g)
extra virgin olive oil, for drizzling

Horseradish salsa verde
50 g fresh white bread,
    crusts removed
2 tablespoons red-wine vinegar
50 g freshly grated horseradish
    (or 1½ tablespoons
    prepared horseradish)
2 cloves garlic, sliced
1 cup chervil leaves
½ cup tarragon leaves
1 cup flat-leaf parsley leaves
125 ml extra virgin olive oil
sea salt flakes and freshly ground
    white pepper

Herb dumplings
150 g suet mix (see page 267)
150 g self-raising flour, plus extra
table salt
⅓ cup mixed chopped flat-leaf
    parsley, tarragon and chives
180 ml cold water

Cypriot lounza with French gherkins and Italian focaccia

Lounza is like a Cypriot version of fresh ham. Unlike other cured meats, it hasn't had all its moisture removed, but it is heavily spiced. Some people make it with beef girello and some use pork loin. I encourage you to make your own, as there is nothing like sitting down to a plate of meat you've cured yourself. However, if you prefer, you can buy it from good Cypriot and Middle Eastern delis. This is a great dish to serve in the middle of the table as a starter before enjoying Gary's Bollito Misto with Herb Dumplings (see page 194).

1 Place wine and salt in a large stainless-steel or glass bowl and stir to dissolve salt.

2 Place pork in a large zip-lock bag, then add cinnamon sticks and pour in half of the wine mixture. Seal bag, taking care to expel any air. Place on a tray or baking dish and refrigerate for 24 hours.

3 Drain wine mixture from bag and discard. Pour in remaining wine mixture and re-seal bag, taking care to expel any air. Refrigerate for another 24 hours.

4 Drain pork, then pat dry with paper towel. Combine cumin and coriander seeds in a shallow baking dish, then roll pork in spices, pressing to coat well. Stand at room temperature, uncovered, for 1 hour.

5 Meanwhile, soak the wood chips in water for 30 minutes. Place three 50 cm-long pieces foil on top each of other on the bench. Drain soaked wood chips, then place in centre of foil. Fold into a parcel, leaving top end open.

6 Have ready 2 grill plates of a four-burner hooded barbecue. Place foil parcel directly onto burners and turn on to low–medium heat, leaving the other burners off. Place pork on a wire rack, then place over wood-chip parcel, close the lid and cook at 130°C for 1½–2 hours or until the core temperature of the pork reaches 70°C on a meat thermometer; check every 30 minutes to make sure the meat isn't drying out. (Alternatively, you can cook the pork in a smoker – in which case, follow manufacturer's instructions.) The cooking time will vary, depending on the thickness of your meat and the type of barbecue used.

7 Remove pork from heat and leave to stand until cool. Wrap in plastic film and refrigerate until chilled.

8 To serve, thinly slice lounza and serve with focaccia, cornichons and a bowl of extra virgin olive oil to the side. Wrap leftover lounza in a clean tea towel and store in fridge for up to 2 weeks.

SERVES 10

focaccia, such as Gary's Focaccia with Chilli Oil (see page 10)
cornichons (see page 266) and extra virgin olive oil, to serve

Lounza
500 ml red wine (shiraz or similar full-bodied red wine)
100 g cooking salt
1.5 kg pork loin (from a large pig for extra fat content), excess sinew trimmed
2 sticks cinnamon
2 tablespoons ground cumin
4 tablespoons coriander seeds, lightly crushed
250 g wood smoking chips (available from large hardware stores)

Lamb

If ever there was a national dish, then lamb has to take credit for being king of the Aussie table. A simple roast leg of lamb with all the trimmings is hard to beat, but it is lamb's versatility and flavour that I love. You can braise the shanks or neck, stuff and pot-roast a shoulder or make a spicy curry from the leg — and then, of course, there's mince, which I've used on page 201 to make fragrant little Moroccan-inspired pies.   GARY

In Greece, interestingly, they don't eat that much lamb at all. When they do, it's usually only small spring lambs of about six to eight kilos in size. Large lambs just aren't eaten. We're blessed here in Australia with really wonderful lamb. I love the secondary cuts, like the neck (which is much underrated). I use lots of it braised in yoghurt, very simply. But there's not much better than a barbecued lamb chop, is there?   George

BASTILLA OF LAMB, OLIVES AND PINE NUTS

George might not tell you, but I laid claim to this recipe of his years ago. The story goes that when he was a lad his mum used to cook open lamb koftas as little snacks (see George's recipe for this on page 202), which are a little different from the fried-egg sandwiches Dad used to cook for me! Here, I've taken the idea of this minced lamb mixture and used it to fill little Moroccan-inspired filo pies – give this recipe a try and then tell me it's not one of the best pies you've ever eaten. You will need to drain the yoghurt in the fridge to thicken it at least a day before you serve this dish.

1 Place the yoghurt on a sheet of muslin, then wrap and suspend over a bowl in the fridge to drain for 24 hours to remove the liquid; the longer you drain it, the thicker it will become. Transfer the yoghurt to an airtight container. Refrigerate for up to 7 days.

2 Heat a large frying pan over medium heat, then add 30 ml of the extra virgin olive oil and cook the lamb mince for 5–8 minutes or until brown, stirring to break up any lumps. Add the onion and garlic and cook for a further 3–4 minutes or until softened. Add the sumac, ground coriander, ground cumin and paprika and cook for a further 2–3 minutes. Season with ½ teaspoon salt and a few twists of pepper, then add the wine and reduce by half. Add the bay leaves, thyme, tomato and stock. Bring to a simmer, then add the olives and half of the coriander. Pop on a lid and cook over low heat for 45 minutes–1 hour, until most of the liquid has evaporated, leaving just enough thick sauce to hold the mixture in the filo pastry.

3 Remove from the heat and add the remaining coriander and all but 3 tablespoons of the pine nuts. Remove the bay leaves and thyme. Leave to cool a little for 10–15 minutes (the filling does not need to be completely cold when you make the pies).

4 Preheat a fan-forced oven to 180°C.

5 Place a sheet of filo on a bench and brush lightly with olive oil. Lay another sheet of filo on top and oil again. Repeat until you have 6 layers. Cut the filo in half widthways to create 2 squares. Repeat the process twice with the remaining pastry to give you 6 squares all up.

6 Brush the inside of 6 round-bottomed 300 ml-capacity ovenproof moulds (rice bowls are ideal, mine are 11 cm × 5 cm) with olive oil, then lay the first square of layered filo into a mould and, using your fingertips, press the pastry gently into the mould. Repeat with the remaining pastry squares and moulds. Divide the lamb mixture between the moulds and gently fold the pastry in towards the centre and over the lamb to seal, trimming the excess. Brush with a little more olive oil and bake for 10 minutes. Turn the pies out of the moulds onto a baking tray lined with baking paper and bake for a further 15 minutes or until golden brown.

7 Smear a generous amount of yoghurt onto 6 plates and drizzle with the remaining extra virgin olive oil, then place a pie in the centre. Sprinkle pine nuts and micro herbs (if using) over the yoghurt, and a little sumac over the pies. Serve immediately.

SERVES 6 AS A MAIN

300 g natural Greek-style yoghurt
150 ml extra virgin olive oil
400 g minced lamb
1 onion, finely chopped
2 cloves garlic, finely chopped
1 tablespoon sumac (see page 267), plus extra for dusting
1 tablespoon ground coriander
2 teaspoons ground cumin
1 teaspoon smoked paprika (see page 267)
table salt and freshly ground white pepper
200 ml dry white wine
2 fresh bay leaves
2 sprigs thyme
2 tomatoes, roughly chopped
200 ml lamb stock or beef stock
75 g kalamata olives, pitted
¼ cup well-washed and chopped coriander, including roots
100 g pine nuts, toasted
18 sheets filo pastry
olive oil, for brushing
micro herbs (optional, see page 267), to serve

Open lamb kofta with cucumber, mint and coriander salad

I cannot take the credit for this dish – it's my mum's. She would have these open koftas ready for us when we came home of an afternoon as a quick snack. Lamb mince is fantastic, especially when made from the shoulder, where there's a good amount of fat. Make these in advance and sit them in the fridge, ready to cook under the griller. In our house there was never any time for the pita base to go soggy – we'd eat them too quickly!

SERVES 4 AS A LIGHT MEAL

1 onion, peeled
1 fresh long red chilli, chopped
1 clove garlic, peeled
olive oil, for cooking
2 tablespoons tomato paste
1 teaspoon ground cumin
1 teaspoon sweet paprika
1 teaspoon ground allspice
500 g minced lamb
2 tablespoons chopped
  flat-leaf parsley
35 g dried breadcrumbs
finely grated zest of 2 lemons
1 tablespoon wholegrain mustard
sea salt flakes
4 x 17–20 cm pita bread rounds
extra virgin olive oil, for brushing
natural Greek-style yoghurt, to serve

Cucumber, mint and
coriander salad
1 handful flat-leaf parsley leaves,
  washed and dried
½ lebanese cucumber, thinly sliced
1 large handful coriander leaves,
  washed and dried
1 large handful mint leaves, washed
  and dried
1 small red onion, thinly sliced
juice of ½ small lemon
50 ml extra virgin olive oil
sea salt flakes

1   Process onion, chilli and garlic in a food processor until finely chopped.

2   Place a wide-based saucepan over medium heat, add a splash of olive oil and cook onion paste until soft, then add tomato paste, cumin, paprika and allspice and cook for a further 1 minute. Set aside to cool.

3   In a large bowl, place minced lamb, parsley, breadcrumbs, lemon zest, mustard and 2 teaspoons sea salt. Mix well. Add onion mixture and mix well.

4   Preheat griller to high.

5   For cucumber, mint and coriander salad, dress parsley, cucumber, coriander, mint and onion with lemon juice, olive oil and sea salt to taste.

6   Place bread on a baking tray and brush with extra virgin olive oil. Spread one-quarter of the lamb mixture evenly over each pita bread, then grill until golden brown, approximately 10 minutes.

7   Season to taste with sea salt, add a dollop of yoghurt, then serve the salad alongside.

Offal

If we are honest, most of us are a little squeamish when it comes to cooking and eating offal. However, if we are to eat meat then we should take the moral high ground and eat every part of the animal. That means eating everything from nose to tail, including the offal. GARY

Most people hate offal, especially livers. But I think the chicken liver parfait (see page 209) is a tasty way to enjoy livers — it is also very high in iron. I'm also a big fan of sweetbreads but not so keen on kidneys. Offal needs to be made flavoursome — it can't be the king — it asks for a lot of sweet and sour, pepper and spice. George

LAMB'S FRY WITH CRISP POTATO AND SAGE

During my school-day lunches, lamb's fry was a nightmare dish for most, braised with onions until it was as dry as an old boot. I still loved it – don't ask me why, I just did. It was a revelation, then, to discover that, simply dusted with a little flour and fried as quick as a flash so it's still pink in the middle, lamb's liver is a knockout. Embellish it with a little sage and lemon and everyone will love it.

SERVES 4 AS A MAIN

1 lamb's liver
80 g unsalted butter, melted,
   plus 30 g extra
1 teaspoon thyme leaves
sea salt flakes and freshly ground
   white pepper
4 potatoes, peeled
2 tablespoons olive oil
2 tablespoons plain flour
12 sage leaves
juice of 1 lemon

1   Remove the thin membrane covering the liver by piercing and then teasing it away with your fingers, effectively peeling the liver. Remove any visible sinew and arteries using the point of a sharp knife, pushing underneath, then lifting the end and cutting away (it may sound a little gruesome, but necessary as these would be chewy when cooked). Cut the liver widthways into 1.5 cm-thick slices to form 8 good-sized steaks. Cover with plastic film and set aside in the fridge.

2   Preheat a fan-forced oven to 190°C.

3   Place the melted butter in a large mixing bowl. Scatter with the thyme and season generously with salt and pepper, then mix.

4   Using a mandoline or large sharp knife, cut the potatoes, starting at the narrowest end, into 1 mm-thick slices. Spread over a baking tray lined with a tea towel and pat dry. Add to the butter mixture and toss to coat well.

5   Place a small square of baking paper in the base of 4 lightly greased 160 ml-capacity metal dariole moulds or 4 holes of a 12-hole metal muffin tray (this will make it easier to remove the potato later). Place the potato slices, one by one, in the moulds; they should sit 1 cm above the rim. Place another square of baking paper on top, then scrunch a large square of foil around the top of the moulds to enclose the potato. Place the moulds on a baking tray and pop into the oven for 40–50 minutes or until the potato is golden on the outside but soft in the middle. Set aside.

6   Heat a non-stick frying pan over high heat and add the olive oil. Dust the liver with a little flour and pat off the excess, then lay the slices in the pan and fry for 2 minutes. Turn over, then immediately add the 30 g extra butter and the sage leaves, season with sea salt and pepper and allow the butter to bubble around the liver for a further 2 minutes until the butter is nut-brown. Add the lemon juice and remove from the heat; the liver should still be pink in the middle.

7   Divide the liver among 4 plates, then spoon over a little of the sage and lemon butter. Run a butter knife around the outside of the potato in each mould, then invert onto the plates and serve.

Chicken liver parfait with samos vin doux jelly

It's very important that all the ingredients for this parfait are at room temperature so that they incorporate and set. Make this parfait well in advance as it gets better over time. Samos vin doux is a sweet wine that comes from the Greek island of Samos. You could use a good sauternes instead. The jelly not only adds a sweet flavour but also protects the parfait from spoiling due to exposure to oxygen. (Without the jelly, the parfait will keep for up to three weeks in the fridge if it's completely covered by melted clarified butter.)

1   Place shallot, garlic, Madeira, port, thyme, bay leaf and peppercorns in a small saucepan and simmer over low heat for 6–7 minutes or until reduced to 60 ml. Remove from heat, then strain through a fine mesh sieve over a bowl, pressing down on solids to extract as much flavour as possible. Discard solids and leave reduction to cool.

2   Meanwhile, melt butter in small saucepan and then leave to reach room temperature.

3   Preheat a fan-forced oven to 120°C.

4   Process livers in a food processor until smooth. Add eggs, one at a time, and process until well combined, then add cooled reduction and salt and combine well. Strain mixture through a fine mesh sieve over a large bowl. Whisk in butter until well combined. If butter sets or curdles mixture, warm bowl very gently over a pan of simmering water, whisking continuously until mixture smooths out.

5   Divide mixture among three 300 ml-capacity ramekins. Line a small baking dish with a piece of cardboard or a tea towel. Place filled ramekins on top and fill pan with enough lukewarm water to come halfway up sides of moulds. Bake for 35–40 minutes or until just set. (The internal temperature should reach 62°C on a meat thermometer.) Remove ramekins from water bath and stand at room temperature for 30 minutes.

6   Meanwhile, for jelly, place Samos vin doux and water in a small saucepan over low heat until just below a simmer, then remove from heat. Place gelatine sheets in a bowl of iced water and soak for 1 minute or until soft. Squeeze out excess water, then add gelatine to wine mixture and stir until dissolved. Strain through a fine mesh sieve, then stand until cool but not set. Pour 50 ml jelly mixture over top of each parfait, then refrigerate for 2 hours or until jelly is firm and set.

7   Serve parfait with slices of toasted baguette.

SERVES 8 AS A STARTER

5 shallots, thinly sliced
1 clove garlic, thinly sliced
100 ml Madeira
100 ml port
3 sprigs thyme
1 fresh bay leaf
5 white peppercorns
250 g unsalted butter, chopped
250 g chicken livers, cleaned
   and all sinew removed
3 free-range eggs, at room
   temperature
1½ teaspoons table salt
toasted baguette, to serve

Samos vin doux jelly
100 ml Samos vin doux
   (a Greek dessert wine)
50 ml water
1½ leaves gold-strength
   gelatine (see page 266)
iced water

Rabbit

Pretty much any recipe that works with chicken is going to work with rabbit. Farmed or wild rabbits are both good, but a farmed rabbit tastes milder and is a good deal plumper. You can buy rabbit from your local butcher and divide it up much like you would a chicken, but unlike our feathered friend it has virtually no fat. Rabbit has a lovely flavour and is a bit of a blank canvas when it comes to splashing on other flavours. The question is, are you prepared to give it a go? GARY

Rabbit is a delicious meat that's lean and healthy, and using it is a great way to get into game as it's not overpowering. I think it's underrated and underutilised here in Australia, which is a shame as we grow some good farmed rabbit. In these recipes I use the legs and Gary uses the rest, so there are no excuses not to give it a go. George

SADDLE OF RABBIT WITH WHITE BEAN PUREE AND HAZELNUT VINAIGRETTE

Okay, so I got a little carried away with this dish. You only need the loin here, so reserve the legs for another use, such as George's risotto on page 215. This is for a special occasion only, and a rehearsal is recommended if you want rave reviews on opening night. For a restaurant-like touch I've garnished this with crisp-fried finely shredded rabbit belly and a grilled rabbit kidney, but the dish still works perfectly without these.

SERVES 4 AS A STARTER

2 rabbits
35 g hazelnuts
6 thin slices flat pancetta
sea salt and freshly ground
    white pepper
olive oil, for cooking
1 teaspoon unsalted butter
1 clove garlic, gently flattened
2 sprigs thyme
nasturtium leaves, rosemary flowers
    and rocket or garlic flowers
    (optional), to serve

White bean puree
100 g dried white beans, such
    as cannellini, soaked in cold water
    for 2 hours, drained
sea salt flakes
125 ml extra virgin olive oil, plus
    extra for drizzling

Hazelnut vinaigrette
80 ml hazelnut oil
100 ml extra virgin olive oil
1 teaspoon chestnut honey
1 teaspoon dijon mustard
finely grated zest and juice
    of 1 lemon
sea salt flakes and freshly
    ground white pepper

1   For the white bean puree, place the drained beans in a saucepan, cover with water and bring to the boil. Reduce the heat to low and simmer for 40 minutes or until just tender. Add a good pinch of salt. Remove from the heat and stand for 5 minutes. Drain, reserving a little of the cooking liquid, then remove one-third of the beans, drizzle with the extra olive oil and set aside. Blend the remaining beans and extra virgin olive oil in a blender until smooth, adding a little of the cooking liquid if necessary to form a smooth puree. Leftover puree will keep in an airtight container in the fridge for up to 3 days.

2   For the vinaigrette, pour the oils into a small bowl and add the honey, mustard, lemon zest and juice. Whisk vigorously for 30 seconds to emulsify, then add a pinch of sea salt and a few twists of pepper and set aside. Leftover vinaigrette will keep in an airtight container in the fridge for up to 2 weeks.

3   To remove the loins and fillets from each rabbit saddle, insert a flexible, sharp, long knife close to the spine, then run the blade gently along the spine to begin to separate the meat from the bone. Continue to tease the rabbit meat away from the bone using the tip of the knife and following the form of the backbone. Remove the small fillets from the underside of the back in the same manner.

4   Preheat a fan-forced oven to 180°C.

5   Roast the hazelnuts on a baking tray for 8 minutes, then transfer to a clean tea towel and rub to remove the skins. Set aside. Place 3 slices of the pancetta slightly overlapping on a chopping board, then place 2 of the loins and 2 of the fillets onto the pancetta, side-by-side, so they sit neatly together. Season with a little sea salt and pepper. Roll the meat in the pancetta to form a tight sausage. Repeat with the remaining pancetta, loins and fillets. Tear off two A4-sized pieces of foil and place them on the bench shiny-side up. Smear with olive oil, then place one rabbit roll at the base of a sheet of foil and roll to form a log. Squeeze ends together and twist to form a tight log. Repeat with the second rabbit roll and sheet of foil.

6   Place the rabbit parcels in a small flameproof roasting pan and roast for 6–8 minutes, then remove and unwrap. Return the rabbit to the pan and add the butter, garlic and thyme sprigs. Cook over medium heat until the butter foams around the rabbit, basting 3 or 4 times with the pan juices, then remove the rabbit from the pan. Slice the rabbit, then serve with the white bean puree and reserved beans, garnished with nasturtium leaves and herb flowers, if desired, and drizzled with hazelnut vinaigrette.

Rabbit and rosemary risotto

The key to this risotto is *not* stirring it; when you stir you can break the grains and make the risotto stodgy. I like to add some soft butter on top to serve – just for Gary! You need to braise the rabbit for a few hours, so that the meat is falling off the bone, before you make the risotto. You could also toss the braised rabbit through pasta or use it as the filling for a luscious pie.

1   Preheat a fan-forced oven to 160°C.

2   For braised rabbit, heat a heavy-based saucepan over medium heat, add olive oil and seal rabbit legs, turning until golden brown, approximately 5 minutes. Transfer to a deep baking dish.

3   Add onion, carrot, celery and garlic to pan and cook over medium–high heat until golden brown, approximately 2–3 minutes. Top rabbits legs with onion mixture, then pour over wine and chicken stock. Add rosemary and thyme. Cover tightly with foil and bake for 1 hour, then remove smaller forelegs and set aside. Cook for another 30 minutes or until meat comes away from bones. Remove from heat, return forelegs to pan and leave meat to cool.

4   Pick meat from bones, discarding bones. Set meat aside. Strain and reserve liquid and discard solids. You will need 1 litre liquid, so add a little extra water if necessary.

5   Heat olive oil in a saucepan over medium heat. Add onion and sweat until translucent, approximately 5–6 minutes. Add rice and cook for 1 minute, stirring constantly.

6   Pour in 500 ml of the reserved rabbit liquid and shake pan (try not to use a spoon to stir rice as it can break grains). When rice has absorbed liquid (8–10 minutes), add another 100 ml rabbit liquid and continue this process with remaining stock, cooking for a further 15 minutes or until rice is al dente. Add rabbit meat, butter, rosemary, chervil and chives and season with sea salt.

7   Serve, scattered with thyme sprigs, if desired.

SERVES 4 AS A MAIN

50 ml olive oil
1 onion, finely chopped
330 g risotto rice, such as
    carnaroli (it's the best!)
60 g unsalted butter, chopped
2 sprigs rosemary, leaves picked,
    finely chopped
2 tablespoons finely
    chopped chervil
2 tablespoons finely chopped chives
sea salt flakes
thyme sprigs (optional), to serve

Braised rabbit
50 ml extra virgin olive oil
1 × 1.5 kg rabbit, jointed, saddle
    reserved for another use
    (such as Gary's saddle of
    rabbit on page 212)
1 onion, roughly chopped
2 carrots, roughly chopped
2 sticks celery, roughly chopped
1 clove garlic, thinly sliced
100 ml white wine
1 litre chicken stock
4 sprigs rosemary
10 sprigs thyme

Veal

I love veal, but I always feel slightly guilty about eating an animal so young that it is essentially a calf, not yet weaned from its mother. We have an ethical responsibility to ensure that all animals reared for our consumption have had as good a life as possible. The veal I buy has been let out to grass and is a little older and the meat a little darker than bobby veal (the male offspring of dairy cows which will not be returned to the herd), which is a 'no-no' at my table. GARY

I didn't grow up eating veal, and to be honest I don't cook it a lot at home. It's milkier than beef and more delicate. However, there are certain cuts that I love using, especially the shank. Veal shank is a great substitute for dishes that call for lamb shank, especially if you don't like the strong, overpowering flavour of lamb. George

VEAL FRICASSEE WITH BROAD BEANS AND PEAS

SERVES 4 AS A MAIN

1 kg boneless veal leg,
    cut into 3 cm pieces

3 litres water

2 tablespoons olive oil

2 onions, sliced

1 head garlic, halved widthways

2 sticks celery, washed, thinly sliced

3 fresh bay leaves

4 sprigs thyme

6 white peppercorns

sea salt flakes

200 ml dry white wine

3 litres chicken stock

300 ml thickened cream

1 tablespoon cornflour

1 tablespoon water

12 white button mushrooms,
    brushed, trimmed

squeeze of lemon juice

800 g fresh broad bean pods
    (to yield 200 g podded beans)
    or 200 g frozen broad beans

500 g fresh pea pods
    (to yield 160 g podded peas)
    or 160 g frozen peas

20 g unsalted butter

tarragon leaves (optional), to serve

An oldie but a goodie. You don't see a lot of white stews or fricassees anymore, which is a shame. The technique is an important one to learn. The secret is to make sure the meat is cooked long enough so it is super-tender (and don't worry about the cream separating – it will be okay). To lighten the fricassee, pour the sauce into a large jug and place the veal and vegetables into serving bowls. Blitz the sauce with a stick blender until light and frothy, then pour over the veal and vegetables and serve.

1 Place the veal in a large heavy-based saucepan or enamelled cast-iron casserole and cover with the water, then bring to the boil over high heat. Remove from the heat and drain in a colander, discarding the water. Rinse the veal under cold water and clean the pan. (This process removes any impurities – such as blood – from the veal, resulting in a lovely white sauce.)

2 Heat the olive oil in the cleaned and dried pan over medium heat for 1 minute. Add the onion, garlic, celery, bay leaves, thyme, peppercorns and 1 teaspoon sea salt and cook for 2 minutes. Add the white wine and simmer until the wine reduces by half. Return the veal to the pan.

3 Add the chicken stock and increase the heat to high. Bring to the boil, then reduce the heat to low and simmer for 1–1½ hours or until the veal is tender, skimming the surface occasionally. Remove from the heat. Remove the veal from the pan and set aside. Strain the stock through a fine mesh sieve over a bowl and discard the vegetables, herbs and spices. Clean the pan, then strain the stock again into the pan. Reduce the stock over high heat for 25 minutes or until you have 600 ml.

4 Add the cream, then bring to the boil and simmer for 3 minutes. Combine the cornflour with the water to make a paste, then add to the boiling sauce. Stir the sauce until it thickens, then simmer for 3 minutes. Return the veal to the pan, add the mushrooms, then simmer for 5 minutes over low heat. Season with a pinch of salt and lemon juice. Set aside.

5 Meanwhile, blanch the podded broad beans and peas in a pan of boiling salted water for 2 minutes, then drain well and toss with the butter.

6 Divide the veal fricassee among 4 bowls, then scatter with the peas, broad beans and tarragon (if using) and serve.

Veal shanks with mastic and yoghurt

This dish needs time — low temperatures and long cooking are the secret to its success. You should be able to eat the meat with a fork, no knife required! What's especially delicious is how the yoghurt turns into a squeaky, tasty cheese when cooked in this way. You don't have to use mastic but it adds a unique flavour. If you can't find mastic oil, use one mastic bead, ground up, instead.

1   Preheat a fan-forced oven to 120°C.

2   Heat olive oil in a heavy-based frying pan over medium–high heat, then add veal shanks and seal, turning until dark and caramelised, approximately 7 minutes. Transfer to a deep roasting pan.

3   Add pearl onions, shallots, onion, leek, mastic, garlic, thyme, wine and lemon zest to roasting pan. Drizzle over honey and pour on chicken stock until veal and vegetables are nearly, but not quite, covered; do not add too much stock to the pan.

4   Spread yoghurt over veal, vegetables and stock, then top with a sheet of baking paper. Cover pan with foil and seal tightly. Bake for 6½–7 hours or until tender. Remove from oven and set aside.

5   Remove veal shanks and yoghurt 'cheese' and keep warm. Strain liquid through a fine mesh sieve into a saucepan, discarding onions and shallots. Simmer over low–medium heat until reduced by three-quarters; this creates the sauce.

6   Pour sauce over veal. Serve veal shanks topped with yoghurt 'cheese' and herbs, if desired.

SERVES 4 AS A MAIN

80 ml olive oil
4 veal shanks (about 650 g each)
6 pearl onions, peeled
6 shallots, peeled
1 red onion, roughly chopped
2 onions, roughly chopped
1 leek, white part only, cleaned
   and cut into 2 cm pieces
5 drops mastic oil or 1 mastic bead
   (see page 267), ground
6 cloves garlic, peeled
6 sprigs thyme
200 ml dry white wine
finely grated zest of 2 lemons
50 g honey (I use Attiki)
1.2 litres chicken stock
   (approximately)
500 g natural Greek-style yoghurt
micro herbs (see page 267) and red
   perilla leaves (optional), to serve

Sardines

ssels

Salmon

FISHMONGER

bster

Oysters

Squid

Prawns

Lobster

There are no two ways about it, crustaceans are expensive.
Lobster, prawns, yabbies and marron all command top dollar.
However, they taste delicious – sweet, succulent and full of flavour.
Lobster turns an ordinary meal into something really special. Make
sure you learn how to use every bit including the shells, which
means you get more bang for your buck. GARY

Crustaceans such as lobster and crayfish are the kings of
the sea. Cook them when you want to be flamboyant and show
off a little bit. I'm just as happy eating lobster simply boiled with
a dollop of creamy homemade mayonnaise as I am eating
it cooked in a fancier way. George

GRILLED LOBSTER WITH FRESH HERBS

Lobster is the ultimate in extravagance. Bring me champagne, caviar and lobster, for I must feast. This dish is a classic that I have cooked for a couple of decades now. The addition of whipped cream and summer herbs just adds an extra flourish.

This recipe will require you to dispatch a lobster. Many people aren't prepared to do this but for those who are, plunging the lobster into boiling water is no longer considered acceptable and certainly not before you render it senseless. I recommend putting the lobster into the freezer for one hour to slow its metabolism. This renders them insensible – you can tell this when they offer no resistance to handling and don't flick back their tail when you stretch it out. Place the lobster on a chopping board, then insert the tip of a sharp, heavy-bladed knife into the centre of the head. Using a strong, single movement, push the knife down into the board, along the front of the head, then split the lobster in two lengthways along the mid-line.

1 Preheat a griller on high.

2 Place the tomatoes still attached to the stems on a baking tray, then sprinkle with the garlic and thyme. Drizzle with extra virgin olive oil and season with salt and a twist of pepper. Place under the griller for 4–5 minutes or until the skins blister and begin to sizzle, then remove from the heat and set aside on the tray.

3 Using a whisk or hand-held electric beaters, whip the cream until soft peaks form. Mix the cream with the herbs and a little sea salt and pepper.

4 Place the lobster halves on a baking tray, flesh-side up, so they sit flat, then season lightly with a little salt and pepper. Spoon the cream mixture liberally over the head and tail flesh of the lobster. Place under the hot griller and grill for 10 minutes or until the cream mixture begins to bubble and turns golden brown. To test if the meat is cooked, pierce the flesh of the tail at the thickest part with the tip of a small sharp knife and see if the flesh is opaque.

5 Remove the lobster from the griller and serve with the blistered tomatoes, scattered with herbs, if desired.

SERVES 2 AS A MAIN

12 vine-ripened cherry tomatoes,
    on the stem
1 clove garlic, thinly sliced
2 sprigs thyme
1½ tablespoons extra virgin olive oil
sea salt flakes and freshly crushed
    black pepper
150 ml thickened cream
2 tablespoons snipped dill
2 tablespoons snipped tarragon
2 tablespoons finely chopped chives
2 tablespoons finely chopped chervil
1 × 800 g raw lobster,
    halved lengthways (see
    recipe introduction)
herb sprigs (optional), to serve

Millionaires' 'moussaka'

I named this dish millionaires' 'moussaka' as it has a number of flamboyant ingredients – namely lobster and caviar. Of course you don't have to be a millionaire to make or eat it – you just have to love food. You can use prawns instead of lobster if you (and your hip pocket) want. Serve this dish with a crisp mixed-leaf salad to the side.

SERVES 2 AS A MAIN

2 bulbs baby fennel, trimmed,
   tops reserved
2 tablespoons olive oil
sea salt flakes
1 carrot, cut into 3 cm pieces
1 onion, cut into 3 cm pieces
2 sticks celery, cut into 3 cm pieces
2 fresh bay leaves
1 lemon, halved
1 orange, halved
1 × 750 g live lobster, humanely
   dispatched (see page 227), shell
   and vein removed, flesh cut into
   5mm-thick slices
ice cubes
2 free-range eggs
6 small kipfler potatoes
caviar (optional), to serve

Bechamel sauce
300 ml milk
3 sprigs thyme
½ clove garlic, bruised
1 wedge onion, sliced
30 g unsalted butter
30 g plain flour
20 g kefalograviera cheese
   (see page 267)

1 Preheat a fan-forced oven to 180°C.

2 Cut fennel into eighths, then place in a roasting pan, pour over olive oil and season with sea salt. Roast until tender, approximately 30 minutes, turning halfway through cooking. Remove and set aside. Reduce oven temperature to 170°C.

3 Fill a large saucepan just over three-quarters with water, then add carrot, onion, celery, bay leaves, lemon, orange and reserved fennel tops. Bring to the boil over high heat and cook for 5 minutes. Add lobster to the pan and cook for 6 minutes. Remove lobster with tongs and place in a sink or bucket of iced water; this stops it from cooking further. Leave in iced water for 5 minutes, then remove and refrigerate.

4 Place eggs in a small saucepan. Cover with cold water and bring to the boil over high heat. Reduce heat to medium, then cook for 3 minutes. Drain then refresh in iced water. Peel and cut into 1 cm-thick slices. Set aside.

5 Place potatoes in a saucepan of cold water and bring to a simmer over high heat, then cook for 10 minutes or until tender. Drain, then slice.

6 For bechamel sauce, place milk in a saucepan and infuse with thyme, garlic and onion over very low heat. Heat until just about to simmer, then remove from heat and leave to infuse for 30 minutes. Heat butter in a heavy-based saucepan over medium heat until melted, then add flour and cook for 2 minutes, stirring constantly with a wooden spoon. Slowly add hot milk, straining it into the pan through a fine mesh sieve and whisking continually so no lumps form. Grate keflagraviera cheese into sauce.

7 Meanwhile, have ready 2 small copper or other ovenproof saucepans (mine are 9 cm wide and 400 ml capacity), then in each one place a layer of potato, a layer of fennel, then a layer of egg. Place 2 slices of lobster on top, then continue this layering process until all potato, fennel, egg and lobster are used, finishing with lobster.

8 Spoon enough bechamel sauce over lobster in each pan to cover. Leftover bechamel sauce can be stored in an airtight container in the fridge for up to 3 days. Bake until golden and heated through, approximately 17–20 minutes.

9 Serve 'moussaka' with a little caviar spooned on top of the bechamel sauce, if desired.

Mussels

When a good friend of mine was a little girl her family spent summers at Port Arlington, on the Bellarine Peninsula in Victoria. Her Italian dad had a tinnie and a long pole with a curved piece of metal and a net at the end. They used to pull up next to the local pier and jetties and run the pole down the pylon to scrape off the mussels that would then fall into the net.
Those clever Italians! GARY

I'm very keen on Spring Bay mussels. Tasmanian waters are the perfect breeding ground for mussels, which need really cold seas to thrive. We're fortunate in Australia to grow some of the best mussels in the world. George

SUGAR-CURED KINGFISH WITH MUSSEL VINAIGRETTE

This recipe ticks all the boxes: sugar- and salt-cured fish; plump, just-cooked mussels; sweet vine-ripened tomatoes; and good-quality extra virgin olive oil. The curing process intensifies and sweetens the flavour of the kingfish — it also works brilliantly with salmon or ocean trout. Prepared this way and sliced thinly, the fish can be eaten as is, drizzled with your favourite extra virgin olive oil and served on warm toast as a little appetiser.

**SERVES 4 AS A STARTER
OR 2 AS A MAIN**

2 star anise
2 teaspoons fennel seeds
1 teaspoon white peppercorns
55 g table salt
55 g caster sugar
finely grated zest of 1 lemon
1 × 500 g kingfish fillet, skin-on,
   pin-boned
olive oil, for cooking
1 tablespoon chervil leaves
micro herbs (see page 267,
   optional), to serve

Mussel vinaigrette
2 vine-ripened tomatoes
boiling water
60 ml extra virgin olive oil
1 large shallot, finely chopped
2 sprigs thyme
1 small clove garlic, chopped
500 g small black mussels
   (sold as cocktail mussels
   from Tasmania), bearded
2 tablespoons dry white wine
squeeze of lemon juice

1 Crush the star anise with a mortar and pestle, then add the fennel seeds and peppercorns and pound lightly together. Reserve 1 teaspoon of this spice mixture. Mix the remainder in a small bowl with the salt, sugar and lemon zest. Sprinkle half of the salt and spice mixture over a stainless-steel, plastic or ceramic tray. Lay the kingfish on the tray and sprinkle the remaining mixture over the top. Cover with plastic film. Refrigerate for 6–8 hours.

2 Wash the salt mixture off the kingfish and pat dry with a clean tea towel or paper towel. Remove the skin and brown flesh from the fillet and thinly slice the kingfish neatly, then set aside.

3 For the mussel vinaigrette, cut a small cross on the base of each tomato, discard the cores and place the tomatoes in a large heatproof bowl. Cover with boiling water and leave for 10 seconds. Drain and rinse the tomatoes with cold water, then peel, halve and remove the seeds. Set aside. Heat a saucepan over high heat. Add a splash of the olive oil and throw in the shallot, thyme and garlic. Cook for 30 seconds, then add the mussels. Add the white wine, pop on a lid and cook for 2–3 minutes. When the mussels have opened, remove the pan from the heat and tip into a strainer over a bowl to collect the juice. Discard any mussels that haven't opened. Return the juices (including the shallot and garlic) to the pan over high heat and reduce by half.

4 Remove half of the mussels from the shells, discarding the shells. Place the mussel meat and the mussels still in their shells in a small bowl, then add the shallot and garlic, discarding the thyme. Drench with the remaining olive oil, then add a little of the cooking juices and the lemon juice. Dice the tomato and add to the mussel mixture.

5 Heat a non-stick frying pan over high heat. Dust the kingfish fillets with a little of the reserved star anise, fennel and pepper mixture, then add a little olive oil to the pan. Sear the fillets quickly for 1½ minutes on each side or until golden on the outside but rare in the centre; the kingfish is cured, so you do not need to cook it through.

6 Divide the kingfish between 2 plates and spoon the mussel vinaigrette over the top. Scatter with the chervil and micro herbs (if using) and serve.

Spring Bay mussel 'spanakopita' with chickpea vinaigrette

This dish is a great little starter for a dinner party. You can also serve it with white anchovies on top, if you like. Spanakopita is a spinach and cheese-filled filo pie, and this recipe originally came about as a way of using up leftover filling in the restaurant. Here I've made just enough to fill the mussels, but if you make a bigger batch of the spanakopita stuffing you'll be able to bake a delicious pie too.

1 For 'spanakopita' stuffing, heat olive oil in a large saucepan and sweat onion and garlic over medium heat until translucent, approximately 4–5 minutes. Add spinach and cook until wilted. Drain well, squeezing out excess moisture. Leave to cool, then roughly chop. Add feta and ricotta cheese and mix well. Season to taste with sea salt. Set aside.

2 Heat vegetable oil in a large heavy-based saucepan over high heat and add mussels. Throw in shallot, garlic and wine. Cover and cook for a few minutes until mussels have opened. Remove mussels from pan and set aside.

3 Strain mussel juices through a colander placed over a bowl, then set aside.

4 Place 1 scant tablespoon 'spanakopita' stuffing inside each mussel, then tie each one firmly closed with kitchen string.

5 Preheat a fan-forced oven to 180°C.

6 Place 100 ml of the mussel juices, chicken stock, tomato, chick peas and onion in a heavy-based ovenproof saucepan large enough to hold the mussels. Add mussels and bring to the simmer, then cover and transfer to oven and cook for 5–8 minutes or until mussels are heated through. Remove kitchen string.

7 Place mussels in a deep serving bowl or individual bowls with hot stock poured over the top. Scatter with micro herbs, if desired. Drizzle with extra virgin olive oil and serve.

SERVES 4–6 AS A STARTER

50 ml vegetable oil
1 kg large Spring Bay mussels, bearded, cleaned
2 shallots, thinly sliced
½ clove garlic, thinly sliced
200 ml dry white wine
300 ml chicken stock
3 tomatoes, seeded, diced
1 × 400 g tin chick peas, drained, rinsed
½ red onion, finely diced
micro herbs (see page 267, optional), to serve
extra virgin olive oil, for drizzling

'Spanakopita' stuffing
50 ml olive oil
1 small onion, finely chopped
1 clove garlic, thinly sliced
300 g baby spinach
80 g feta, crumbled
80 g firm ricotta cheese
sea salt flakes

Oysters

I never used to like oysters — it was always a textural thing rather than a dislike of the flavour. Now I have a love for them, born from an appreciation of where and how they are farmed and where they sit in the food chain — they are bivalve molluscs, the filters of the ocean, and barometers of the ocean's health. Oysters are, of course, an aphrodisiac, so even if you're not a fan, you're obliged to partake of them once in a while, then you'll grow to love them just like I have. GARY

We are so blessed in this country with great oysters. My issue with oysters is that they must be shucked to order and eaten immediately. If you are afraid to shuck them yourself get your fishmonger to do it in front of you and tell them to leave the lids on so you don't lose any of the natural juices. Then serve them as soon as you get home! George

FRESHLY SHUCKED OYSTERS WITH BLACK-BEAN VINAIGRETTE

SERVES 4 AS A STARTER

1 tablespoon salted Chinese black
  beans (see page 266), soaked
  in water for 1 hour
60 ml peanut oil
4 cloves garlic, finely chopped
1 small fresh red chilli,
  finely chopped
1 teaspoon finely chopped ginger
2 tablespoons caster sugar
60 ml coconut vinegar
  (see page 266)
1 teaspoon sesame oil
pinch of Japanese mustard powder
300 g rock salt
24 oysters, unshucked
¼ small daikon, shredded
1 small handful baby perilla
  or coriander
2 spring onions, shredded

Oysters are best bought as fresh as you can get them, closed and from a reputable seafood supplier. The biggest problem with buying them open is that you lose all the lovely juice or liquor inside, which has that slight taste of iodine, and is salty and fresh just like the sea. After all, it is this very taste that oyster lovers adore! Shucking an oyster isn't that hard once you have learnt how and, contrary to popular thought, it is not about brute force but more about a tease and a twist. For this dish (pictured over the page), I use Japanese mustard powder (karashi powder). It has a strong, rich mustard flavour and is available from Asian food stores. Baby perilla is a member of the mint family and one of my favourite herbs.

1 Drain the black beans and set aside on paper towel.

2 Heat 1½ tablespoons of the oil in a wok or small non-stick frying pan over low heat for 1 minute. Fry the garlic for 2 minutes, taking care not to brown. Increase the heat to medium and add the black beans, then cook for 2 minutes or until the black beans become fragrant and soft. Add the chilli and ginger and stir, then add the sugar and vinegar and cook for 1 minute, stirring until the sugar has dissolved.

3 Tip the black bean mixture into a small bowl. Add the remaining peanut oil and the sesame oil and mustard powder and stir to combine.

4 Sprinkle 4 plates or a platter with rock salt as a bed for the oysters; this prevents them from falling over and losing their precious liquor.

5 Carefully shuck the oysters with an oyster knife by inserting the point of the knife into the gap between the top and bottom shell at the hinge. Twist and pop the hinge. Remove the top (flat) shell carefully, making sure you separate the top shell from the oyster and ensuring that you retain the juice.

6 Divide the oysters among the 4 plates or platter; try to keep them stable and upright. Spoon a little of the dressing over each of the oysters, then top with a small bundle of daikon, a sprig of perilla or coriander and some spring onion. Serve immediately.

Freshly shucked oysters with ginger and mountain tea vinaigrette

Mountain tea (*Syderitis syriaka*) is a wild plant that grows in the mountains all over Greece. It has strong medicinal properties – it's great for sore tummies – and is readily available in Greek delis. Heating the leaves brings out the flavour. The honey dressing for the oysters (pictured over the page), will need to be started at least one day ahead of serving to allow the flavours to develop.

SERVES 4 AS A STARTER

200 ml honey (I use Attiki)
2 tablespoons extra virgin olive oil
50 ml white-wine vinegar
2 star anise
20 g young ginger, peeled
2 teaspoons fish sauce
juice of ½ lime
2 teaspoons water
1 tablespoon mountain tea leaves and flowers
16 oysters (whatever variety is good and in season), unshucked

1   Heat 100 ml of the honey and the extra virgin olive oil in a small saucepan over low heat. Whisk in vinegar and add star anise. Bring to a simmer, then set aside and leave to cool.

2   Meanwhile, slice ginger as finely as possible using a mandoline or a very sharp knife. Place ginger in a pan, cover with cold water and bring to the boil, then drain. Repeat this process 3 times – this will help to remove bitterness and reduce intensity of ginger. Add ginger to honey and vinegar mixture, cover with plastic film and leave to pickle for at least 1 day; the longer the better.

3   Gently heat remaining honey in a saucepan over low heat until warmed. Add fish sauce, lime juice and water, then add mountain tea leaves and flowers.

4   Remove ginger from honey and vinegar mixture and finely shred, then add to mountain tea mixture. Refrigerate until chilled.

5   Freshly shuck oysters (see opposite) and serve with strained ginger and mountain tea vinaigrette poured over. Any leftover vinaigrette can be stored in an airtight container in the fridge for a few months.

Prawns

When I lived in England a prawn was a little thing — often bought frozen and so watery with no great flavour — that you had in your prawn cocktail. How lucky we are here in Oz. Our prawns are huge with plump and textured flesh. Make sure you buy sulphur-free Aussie prawns, support our local industry — and throw one or two on the barbie for me! GARY

We farm some amazing prawns in this country and with some clever cooking techniques you can make some fabulous dishes with them. Don't be afraid to use the heads — they've got so much flavour. Simply fry the prawn heads until they are crisp. The shells are great for stocks, bisques and soups. While Gary shows us how to make a delicate prawn ravioli (see page 239), on page 240 I show how to simply bake them with a smothering of homemade hummus. George

PRAWN MOUSSE RAVIOLI

Prawns make the perfect seafood-based mousse. Firstly, they are very high in protein so the mousse is firm and smooth, giving an exquisite texture and mouthfeel when cooked. Secondly, the prawn meat is deliciously sweet and, in this recipe, the wholegrain mustard adds a savouriness and bite to the supple ravioli.

1   Shred 100 g of the prawn meat, then place in a bowl, cover with plastic film and put into the fridge. Process the remaining 200 g prawn meat with ¼ teaspoon salt and cayenne in a food processor until a paste forms. Add the egg white and blend until the mixture is smooth. Add 60 ml of the cream and mix using the pulse button to avoid over-mixing. Add the remaining cream and pulse again several times to incorporate. Transfer the mousse to a bowl, then add the lemon zest. Cover with plastic film and refrigerate for at least 30 minutes to become firm.

2   For the pasta dough, blend the flour, salt and eggs in a food processor until combined. Add the oil and water and blend until the mixture has a fine and moist crumb-like consistency. Turn the dough out onto a lightly floured bench and knead into a ball; it should be cohesive, smooth and elastic. Press the dough down to flatten and form a rough rectangle. Wrap in plastic film and leave to rest for 30 minutes.

3   Sprinkle a little flour on the bench and unwrap the dough, then cut it in half. Using a rolling pin lightly dusted with flour, roll and elongate one half into a rectangle so that it will pass through the first setting of the pasta machine more easily.

4   Feed the dough through the rollers of a pasta machine set at the widest setting, turning the handle and teasing the rolled dough along the bench as it feeds through the machine. Brush the flour off the pasta sheet, then fold one end over onto the centre and press it down. Fold the other end over the top and press it down, then feed the dough through the machine on the same setting. Repeat this process twice. Fold the dough and feed it through the rollers, reducing the setting each time, making the dough thinner, until you reach the second-last setting. Transfer the pasta sheet to a lightly floured baking tray, then cover with a tea towel and repeat with the remaining piece of dough and cover this too.

5   Transfer the mousse to a piping bag fitted with a 1.5 cm plain nozzle and set aside. Place the water and egg yolk in a small bowl and set aside.

6   Lightly flour the bench and lay one of the pasta sheets on top, leaving the other half covered so it doesn't dry out. Pipe twelve 4 cm-wide × 3 cm-high mounds of the mousse onto the pasta sheet in two zig-zagging rows about 3–4 cm apart. Using a pastry brush, brush the beaten egg yolk mixture around the mousse, then cover with the remaining pasta sheet. Press the top sheet of pasta down around the mousse with your hands, gently squeezing out any air pockets. Using a plain cutter large enough to fit around the mousse (use the cutter upside-down so you can press the dough together to encase the mousse), stamp out the ravioli and place on a semolina-dusted tea towel. Leave in an airy, dry spot for 30 minutes, turning once, to dry out. >

SERVES 4–6 AS A STARTER

650 g raw prawns, peeled (shells retained for making the Prawn Oil on page 58) and cleaned (to yield about 300 g prawn meat)
sea salt flakes
pinch of cayenne pepper
1 free-range egg, separated
125 ml thickened cream
finely grated zest and juice of ½ lemon
½ teaspoon water
180 ml Prawn Oil (see page 58)
2 tablespoons wholegrain mustard
micro herbs (see page 267, optional), to serve

Pasta dough
200 g strong plain flour (see page 266), plus extra for dusting
pinch of table salt
2 × 55 g free-range eggs
2 teaspoons olive oil
2 teaspoons water
semolina, for dusting

7   Bring a large saucepan of water to the boil over high heat. Add a pinch of salt and place the ravioli in the boiling water. Reduce the heat to low and simmer for 3–4 minutes or until the ravioli are nice and firm. Remove with a slotted spoon to drain on paper towel. Keep warm.

8   Meanwhile, warm the prawn oil in a small saucepan over medium heat for 2 minutes; do not let it boil or it will lose its lovely flavour. Add the mustard, 1 teaspoon of the lemon juice and the shredded prawn meat, then season with a pinch of salt and stir. Remove from the heat and stand for 2–3 minutes off the heat, allowing the residual heat to cook the prawn meat. Add lemon juice to taste.

9   Place 2 or 3 ravioli on each plate or shallow bowl and spoon over the warm mustard and prawn oil vinaigrette, then scatter with micro herbs (if using) and serve.

Prawns baked in hummus with toasted almonds

SERVES 4 AS A MAIN

50 g flaked almonds
12 large raw prawns, peeled and
    cleaned, heads and tails intact,
    intestinal tracts removed

Hummus
1 × 400 g tin chick peas,
    drained, rinsed
3 cloves garlic, roughly chopped
2 tablespoons tahini
80 ml lemon juice
100 ml extra virgin olive oil
1 teaspoon ground cumin
1 teaspoon sea salt flakes

I adore hummus. It's one of those dips that you can actually heat up and it won't separate. Baked with prawns it's just delicious: the almonds are crunchy, the prawn meat is beautifully sweet and the dish is super easy. The flavours combine well – none are too dominant – and the hummus adds both flavour and richness.

1   For hummus, blend chick peas, garlic and tahini in a blender or food processor. Slowly add lemon juice, then olive oil. Season with cumin and salt. Makes approximately 800 ml. Any leftover hummus can be stored in an airtight container in the fridge for 3–4 days.

2   Preheat a fan-forced oven to 160°C.

3   Place almonds on a baking tray and roast until golden brown, approximately 10–12 minutes.

4   Increase the oven temperature to 170°C. Spoon a layer of hummus into the base of 1 or 2 baking dishes just large enough to hold prawns in a single layer. Place prawns evenly over hummus, then spoon more hummus over prawns; but don't cover the heads.

5   Bake until prawns are just cooked through, approximately 12–13 minutes. Sprinkle with flaked almonds and serve.

Salmon

How wealthy are we? Fifty years ago you would have had to be absolutely loaded to enjoy salmon and a glass of sparkling wine for lunch! Now widely available, salmon is a beautiful fish, soft, ever so rich and jammed full of omega-3 fatty acids. There are few fish as easy to cook as salmon that also give such fantastic results. GARY

I've been lucky to cook wild salmon several times and it's an amazing fish. The farmed salmon that we get here is quite different, with a specific flavour, but it's readily available from fishmongers and supermarkets. Salmon is a versatile, oily fish. Serve it raw, roasted, pan-fried or as a confit – the possibilities are endless. Ocean trout can be used in place of salmon in most recipes, if you prefer. George

ROASTED SALMON WITH OXTAIL SAUCE

A number of classic fish dishes include a rich meaty sauce featuring ingredients such as bacon, mushrooms and shallots; ordinarily, what you would expect with, say, a fillet steak. Trust me, this is the best 'surf and turf' you are ever likely to try. Oxtail makes the richest of red-wine sauces that, when served in generous amounts with crisp-skinned salmon, is heavenly. Now, where's the bread to mop up all that sauce?

SERVES 4 AS A MAIN

1 For the oxtail sauce, place the oxtail, wine, carrot, celery, onion, garlic, bay leaves and thyme in a large stainless-steel or glass bowl. Cover with plastic film and refrigerate for 24 hours.

2 Preheat a fan-forced oven to 165°C.

3 Remove the oxtail from the bowl and pat dry with paper towel, then set aside. Strain the red-wine marinade into a saucepan and bring to the boil over high heat, skimming any impurities from the surface, then strain through a muslin-lined sieve into a bowl. Separate the bay leaves and thyme from the vegetables and set both aside.

4 Heat the olive oil in an enamelled cast-iron casserole over a medium heat, then lightly season the oxtail with salt and pepper. Cook for 10 minutes or until brown on all sides. Remove from the pan and set aside. Add the reserved vegetables and cook for 8 minutes or until caramelised, stirring occasionally.

5 Add the thyme, bay leaves and red wine to the pan, then bring to the boil over high heat and reduce the wine by two-thirds. Add the oxtail and veal stock and bring to the boil. Pop on a lid, then transfer to the oven and cook for 2½ hours or until the oxtail is tender. Remove from the oven. Carefully remove the oxtail from the pan and set aside. The meat should fall off the bone in pieces when you push it with a fork. Leave to cool for 10 minutes so it is cool enough to handle. Remove the meat from the bones and set aside.

6 Strain the sauce through a fine mesh sieve over a bowl. Return the sauce to the clean, dry pan. Bring to the boil over medium heat; adjust the seasoning. The sauce should be slightly viscous and glossy but not sticky. Add the meat to the sauce and heat through.

7 Place one salmon fillet, flesh-side up, on a chopping board. Season lightly with sea salt and pepper. Lay the other fillet, flesh-side down, on top (in a sense, you are reassembling the salmon, having removed all the bones). Slide kitchen string around the centre of the fish and tie the 2 pieces together firmly, securing with a single knot. Repeat tying the fish fillets together securely with kitchen string at 1 cm intervals. Season well with salt and pepper. Heat a large heavy-based non-stick frying pan over medium heat. Add the extra virgin olive oil and heat until it shimmers. Gently place the salmon in the pan and cook for 2 minutes on each side or until light-golden brown. Add the garlic and thyme, then roast in the oven for 4 minutes, turn and roast for another 4 minutes; the salmon will be medium–rare. Transfer the salmon to a plate and leave to rest for 2 minutes.

8 Divide the oxtail sauce among 4 bowls and place a slice of the salmon fillet on top, then serve, perhaps with some nice mashed potato or steamed green vegetables to the side. Leftover oxtail sauce can be stored in an airtight container in the fridge for up to 5 days or freezer for up to 1 month. It makes a delicious sauce for pasta such as pappardelle.

2 × 400 g salmon fillets, centre-cut,
    skin on and pin-boned
sea salt flakes and freshly ground
    black pepper
2 tablespoons extra virgin olive oil
1 clove garlic, thinly sliced
2 sprigs thyme
mashed potato and steamed green
    vegetables (optional), to serve

Oxtail sauce
8 pieces oxtail, fat trimmed
750 ml red wine
1 carrot, cut into 1 cm dice
1 stick celery, cut into 1 cm dice
1 onion, cut into 1 cm dice
4 cloves garlic, peeled
2 fresh bay leaves
4 sprigs thyme
40 ml olive oil
table salt and freshly ground
    white pepper
750 ml good-quality veal
    or beef stock

Salmon poached in olive oil with tomato butter sauce

SERVES 4 AS A MAIN

250 g cherry tomatoes
2 tablespoons tomato sauce
pinch of sea salt flakes
50 g soft unsalted butter
1 litre extra virgin olive oil
4 salmon fillets (about 160 g each),
   skin removed

As you've probably realised by now, I'm an olive oil freak! This buttery tomato sauce is really easy to make. It's fairly idiot-proof – just make sure you don't boil it or it will split. Keep your eye on the salmon as it cooks in the olive oil at a low temperature – you don't want to overcook it. A candy thermometer is a worthwhile investment for your gadget drawer; however, if you don't have one, keep a close eye on both the sauce and the salmon as they should not get too hot. You could always brush the fish with a bit of olive oil and roast it in a hot oven for about twelve minutes instead. I've added olive leaves to the olive oil here (see opposite), however, this is not necessary.

1   Blend tomatoes, tomato sauce and salt in a blender until smooth. Pass sauce through a fine mesh sieve into a small saucepan. Heat sauce gently over low heat until it registers 60°C on a candy thermometer; do not boil. Blend in butter using a stick blender.

2   Heat olive oil in a saute pan or deep frying pan over low heat until it registers 50°C on a candy thermometer, then add salmon. Cook for 17 minutes or until centre is translucent; the oil needs to be brought back up to 50°C after salmon has been added, so keep an eye on the temperature and adjust timing if necessary.

3   Remove salmon from olive oil and serve with tomato butter sauce.

Sardines

When you think of the Mediterranean, you have to think of sardines. The romantic in me sees little wooden fishing boats worn by time and toil, and old weather-beaten men pulling in nets laden with a wriggly blanket of silvery-blue sardines. Here's to days gone by . . . and to the humble sardine. GARY

Sardines are a quintessential Greek ingredient – just think about all those beautiful islands! Some islands even have their own annual sardine festivals. I've eaten sardines all my life and I just love them. Don't be afraid to leave the heads on and eat them too, as there are some juicy flavours within. George

SARDINE AND GREEN TOMATO TOASTS

If you don't eat a lot of oily fish such as mackerel or sardines, it can be a 'fishy' business cooking with them for the first time. There are a couple of ways to get over this. Firstly, make sure you are using super-fresh fish; sardines get fishier over a period of a few days. Secondly, combine them with strong acidic or sweet ingredients that complement their flavour. We should try to eat more oily fish – they are jam-packed full of omega-3s, and these toasts (pictured over the page) are a great recipe to get you started.

SERVES 4 AS A STARTER OR SNACK

1 thin sourdough baguette
60 ml extra virgin olive oil, plus
    extra for brushing
1 clove garlic, peeled, halved
1 avocado, halved, stone
    removed, peeled
3 small green tomatoes, halved,
    thinly sliced
12 sardine fillets
sea salt flakes and freshly ground
    black pepper
finely grated lemon zest (optional)
    and lemon wedges, to serve

1 Preheat a fan-forced oven to 160°C.

2 Slice the baguette thinly on a 45-degree angle to produce long oval slices. Brush the bread lightly with a little extra virgin olive oil on each side, then place on a baking tray and pop into the oven for 6 minutes or until golden and crisp. Remove from the oven and rub the garlic over one side of the toasts, then set aside.

3 Slice the avocado thinly, then lay avocado and tomato slices side by side on each toast, overlapping slightly. Set aside.

4 Heat a non-stick frying pan over high heat and add 2 tablespoons of the extra virgin olive oil to the pan. Gently lay the sardines skin-side down in the pan, then reduce the heat to medium and cook for 2–3 minutes until light golden. There is no need to cook the sardines on the other side as they are so thin and delicate. Remove from the pan and place 1 fillet on each of the toasts.

5 Drizzle with the remaining extra virgin olive oil, sprinkle with a little sea salt and season with a twist of pepper, then top with a little grated lemon zest (if using). Serve with wedges of lemon to the side.

Sardine 'saganaki' with bruised tomatoes

For me this dish (pictured over the page) is all about quick cooking. The fish crisp up nicely on the outside, and the sauce adds the classic Mediterranean flavours of tomato, garlic and parsley. Traditionally, the term 'saganaki' refers to a pan used for frying seafood such as prawns or mussels. Just promise me when you cook these sardines that you'll grab a little glass with some ouzo and ice and think of me!

1 Preheat a fan-forced oven to 180°C.

2 Place 80 ml of the extra virgin olive oil in a heavy-based ovenproof frying pan over high heat. Add sardines to pan and seal on both sides, approximately 1–2 minutes. Transfer pan to oven and cook for 5 minutes or until just cooked through. Remove sardines to a serving plate.

3 Heat an enamelled cast-iron or heavy-based frying pan over high heat for 2–3 minutes, then add remaining olive oil, tomatoes, shallot and garlic and cook for 1 minute. Add sherry vinegar, then remove from heat and season with salt.

4 Spoon tomato mixture over sardines and serve, scattered with crumbled feta and mint.

SERVES 4 AS A LIGHT MEAL OR STARTER

230 ml extra virgin olive oil
12 sardines, cleaned, scaled
250 g cherry tomatoes
4 shallots, thinly sliced
1 clove garlic, thinly sliced
2 tablespoons sherry vinegar
1 teaspoon sea salt flakes
feta, crumbled, and mint leaves, to serve

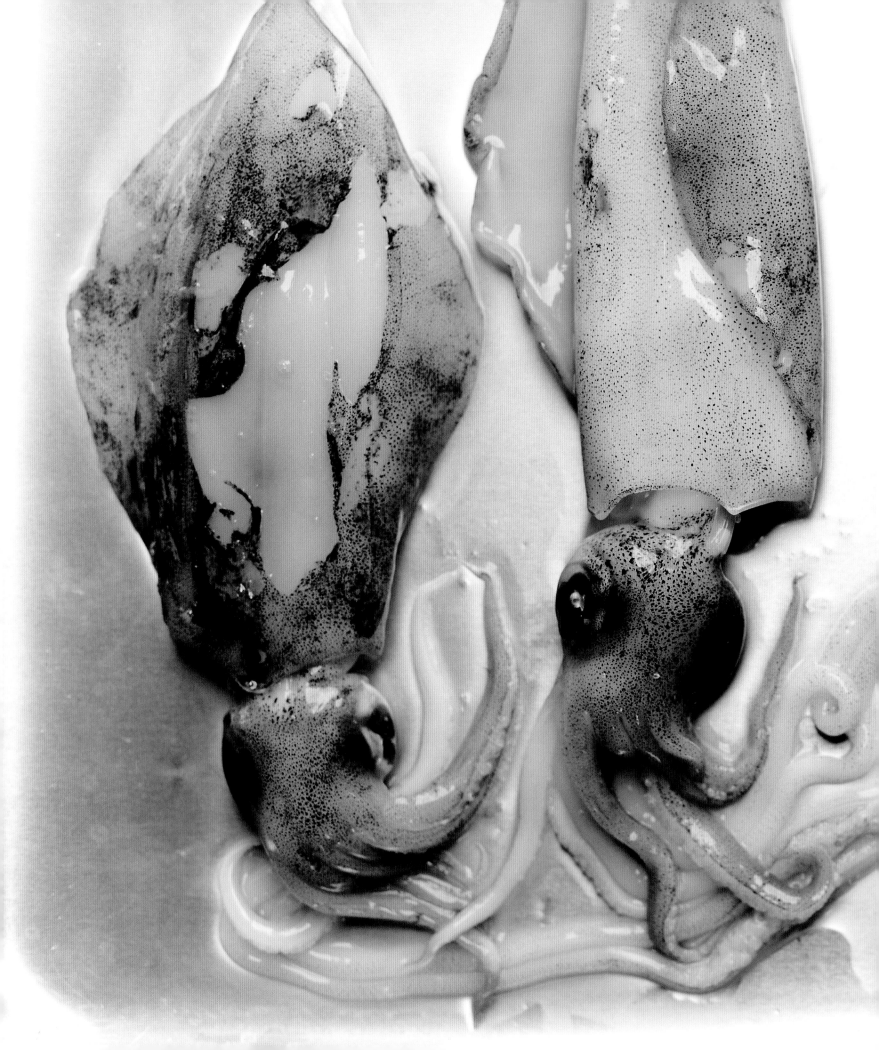

Squid

Not that many years ago no Anglo-Saxon would ever think of eating squid, calamari or cuttlefish – a poor man's catch or, worse, bait. When these did appear in the fish and chip shop or across the pub counter it was most often deep-fried straight from the freezer, heavily crumbed and flavourless. How things have changed. Remember the 'tender – tough – tender' rule with squid and octopus. Cook quickly and it will be tender, as you cook it further it becomes tougher until finally, cooked over a long time such as in a braise or stew, it becomes tender again. GARY

I absolutely love Gary's take on salt-and-pepper squid (see page 263) and I would choose it over my recipe (see page 264) any day, although mine is the healthier option of the two! Squid is great as it only needs to be cooked quickly to be delicious. If you cook it too much it will toughen. On the flip-side, what's also great about squid is that you can braise it slowly for a long period of time in red wine, which is very nice too. George

SQUID WITH CHILLI, GARLIC AND CRISP LETTUCE

There is a little restaurant in the Vietnamese stronghold of Victoria Street in Melbourne's Richmond that serves the best salt-and-pepper squid. It's not so much about the salt or the pepper but the chilli and the crispy fried nibs of garlic. It is gorgeous – slightly sweet, salty, crisp, crunchy and intensely garlicky, with a hit of chilli heat at the end. Pow! That's what I'm talkin' about. Here's my take on this classic dish.

1   Rinse the squid, then separate the hood and tentacles. Rinse and remove the contents of each hood and rinse again. Remove the head and beak from the tentacles and rinse again. Remove the quill from inside the hoods and discard. Score each hood lightly on the softer side on the diagonal with the tip of a sharp knife then repeat in the other direction to form a neat criss-cross pattern. Cut each hood into 4 cm pieces and set aside with the tentacles.

2   Heat a splash of the oil in a wok over low heat and fry the garlic until just golden. Remove the garlic with a slotted spoon and transfer to paper towel to drain, then set aside.

3   Mix the cornflour, rice flour, salt and pepper in a bowl and set aside. Place the egg white in a stainless-steel bowl, then beat until light and foamy. Place the squid first into the egg white, then lift out, wipe off the excess and toss through the flour mixture. Set aside.

4   Heat oil for deep-frying in a large, deep, heavy-based saucepan until it registers 185°C on a candy thermometer. Working in batches if necessary, deep-fry the squid for 4 minutes or until crisp, then remove with a slotted spoon and drain on paper towel.

5   Heat a splash of extra oil in the wok and fry the spring onion, chilli and ginger for a few seconds over medium heat, then add the squid and coriander and toss together. Tip the lot onto a plate and serve with the lettuce, cucumber and coriander sprigs.

SERVES 4 AS A STARTER

2 squid (about 400 g each)
500 ml peanut oil, for deep-frying, plus a little extra
1 head garlic, finely chopped
35 g cornflour
75 g rice flour
2 teaspoons sea salt flakes
2 teaspoons freshly ground white pepper
1 free-range egg white
2 spring onions, thinly sliced
2 fresh red bird's-eye chillies, thinly sliced
2 fresh green bird's-eye chillies, thinly sliced
1 fresh long red chilli, thinly sliced
2 teaspoons finely chopped ginger
2 tablespoons chopped coriander
1 small iceberg lettuce, washed, leaves separated
2 small lebanese cucumbers, peeled, cut into strips
coriander sprigs, to serve

Warm salad of squid with chick peas and wild greens

In Greece during Lent you traditionally wouldn't eat seafood containing any blood, so squid was very popular at that time of year. It goes really well with the lentils, chick peas, vinegar and olive oil here to make a really healthy, tasty dish. To dress it up a little, I garnish it with baby mache.

SERVES 4 AS A STARTER OR LIGHT MEAL

2 small squid (about 200 g each)

1 carrot, quartered

1 onion, quartered

1 stick celery, quartered

80 g dried Puy-style green lentils

1 fresh bay leaf

1 litre cold water

50 ml extra virgin olive oil, plus extra for drizzling

6 leaves (½ bunch) Tuscan black cabbage (cavolo nero), washed, trimmed, cut into 4 cm lengths

375 g (½ bunch) endive, washed, trimmed, cut into 4 cm lengths

110 g (½ bunch) amaranth, washed, trimmed, cut into 4 cm lengths

2 tomatoes, cut into 5 mm dice

90 g tinned chick peas, drained, rinsed

1 tablespoon sherry vinegar

sea salt flakes

baby mache (lamb's lettuce, optional), to serve

1   To clean squid, remove tentacles and all parts inside tubes, including head, beak and quill, then rinse well. Reserve tentacles for another use. Cut tubes into 2 cm pieces. Set aside.

2   Put carrot, onion, celery, lentils and bay leaf into a saucepan. Cover with the cold water, then simmer over low heat until lentils are tender, approximately 40 minutes. Drain, removing and discarding vegetables.

3   Place extra virgin olive oil in a large frying pan over high heat. Add squid and fry for 3 minutes or until golden brown, then add all the greens and cook for 1 minute or until wilted. Add lentils, tomato and chick peas and fry for another 1 minute. Add sherry vinegar and drizzle with a little more extra virgin olive oil.

4   Season to taste with sea salt, then scatter with mache, if desired. Transfer to plates or shallow bowls and serve.

Glossary

Black beans – salted Chinese These salted preserved soy beans blacken and soften during the fermentation process. They are a key ingredient in black bean sauce and add a salty, bittersweet note to dishes. Available from Asian food stores.

Bonito flakes Bonito fish is related to mackerel and tuna. The filleted fish is dried until rock hard, then shaved into strongly fragrant flakes and used as a garnish, as well as to make dashi (see this page). Available from Asian food stores.

Butter – clarified To clarify butter, pop unsalted butter into a microwave-safe container and microwave on a medium setting for 90 seconds. Remove and allow the milk solids and butterfat to separate. Skim off the butterfat and reserve, discarding the milk solids.

Caperberries The edible bud and fruit of the caper bush, preserved in vinegar. Available from specialty food stores.

Chinese sausage (*lap cheung*) A sweet, red, dried pork sausage. There are several different varieties. They are quite hard and tight but develop a lovely flavour when sliced and steamed, grilled or fried on their own or as part of more complex dishes. Available from Asian food stores and larger supermarkets.

Chocolate – dark couverture The best chocolate that you can find is couverture. It must by law contain a minimum of thirty-two per cent cocoa butter and fifty-four per cent combined total of cocoa solids and cocoa butter. The more cocoa butter and solids a chocolate contains, the less sugar and the more flavour it has. Cooking chocolate on the other hand contains a lot more sugar, vegetable oils and often artificial flavourings.

Coconut vinegar A cloudy, white vinegar made from fermented coconut water (the liquid inside young coconuts). It adds a sharp note to dishes. Available from Asian food stores.

Cornichons Also known as gherkins or French cornichons, these are young cucumbers pickled in vinegar or brine and herbs. Available from specialty food stores and good delis.

Dashi powder A Japanese stock powder made from either bonito flakes (see this page), shiitake mushrooms or kombu (dried kelp). It is the base for many great Japanese dishes, so take care to buy a good brand. Spiral Foods make dashi without MSG, which is worth looking out for.

Flour – strong plain Bread-making requires a strong, elastic flour that can absorb a high level of liquid to produce a dense, chewy dough capable of expanding without collapsing as the yeast goes to work. 'Strong' refers to the amount of gluten in the flour. '1–0' and '00' flour are grades of flour milled and exported from Italy. The grading indicates how fine the flour is, as well as how much bran and wheat germ have been removed. '00' is a super-fine flour; the high-protein or strong '00' flours are suitable for making bread and pizza.

Freekeh Made from green wheat harvested while still young, then sun-dried and carefully set on fire to separate the straw and chaff from the seeds, before being roasted and thrashed to crack into smaller pieces. Popular throughout the Middle East, freekeh has a nutty flavour. Wholegrain and cracked freekeh are available from specialty food stores and health food stores.

Gelatine leaves Available as titanium, platinum or gold strength, gelatine leaves are pure and easy to use. Commercial kitchens generally avoid using powdered gelatine because leaf gelatine has better setting properties so the results are more predictable. Available from specialty food stores and good delis.

Glucose – liquid A 'single' sugar in the form of syrup commonly used in commercial kitchens for making ice cream, sorbet and confectionery. It often replaces a proportion of white sugar in recipes. Available from health food stores.

Gluten Gluten can be added to the dough for bread or pizza to increase its chewiness. Available from specialty food stores.

Haloumi A Cypriot-style cheese traditionally made from goat's and sheep's milk. It has a high melting point, making it suitable for grilling and frying. Available from good delis and larger supermarkets.

Kefalograviera Originating in Greece, this hard, salty cheese is traditionally made from sheep's milk and is commonly used for cooking, although it is also appreciated as a table cheese. Available from Greek food stores and good delis.

Manouri This Greek semi-soft, whey-based cheese is usually made from sheep's or goat's milk. It has a mild, often lemony flavour and a creamy texture. Available from Greek food stores and good delis.

Mastic The hardened, opaque resin from the *Pistacia lentiscus chia* plant, an evergreen tree that grows in Chios, Greece. Mastic is used in Greek baking, sweets, drinks and ice cream. Available from Greek food stores, good delis and *herbies.com.au*.

Micro herbs Baby herbs have recently become popular with chefs as a way of adding subtle flavours. Available from specialty greengrocers.

Mirin A sweet, delicate Japanese rice wine exclusively used for cooking. Available from Asian food stores and supermarkets.

Miso – brown rice A fermented soy-bean paste flavoured with brown rice. Available from Asian food stores, health food stores and larger supermarkets.

Mushrooms – king brown These large, stout edible fungi have short gills and a thick, meaty stem that tastes just as delicious as the fleshy caps.

Ovens The recipes in this book were tested using a fan-forced oven. If using a conventional oven, check your manufacturer's instructions and increase the oven temperature (usually 20°C higher for a non fan-forced oven), and adjust the cooking time accordingly. Always preheat your oven well before baking or roasting.

Paprika – smoked Increasingly popular, this deep-red spice is made from capsicums that are slowly smoked over oak, and is sold in three varieties – hot, bittersweet and sweet. Used sparingly, it adds a fantastic smoky and complex flavour. The best brands, such as La Chinata, come from La Vera in Spain. Available from specialty food stores and good delis.

Rice paper – confectionery Commonly used in making confectionery, this is a thin, edible paper that is not actually made from rice. Available from larger supermarkets.

Rigani (mountain oregano) Also known as Greek oregano, this is the dried and cut flower tops and leaves of the *Origanum vulgare* subspecies of herb belonging to the mint family. Available from Greek food stores and good delis.

Rock sugar – yellow A dark yellow sugar that is a crystallised form of a mixture of honey, refined and unrefined sugars. Available from Asian food stores and supermarkets.

Salt – flaked black sea This mineral salt is available in large crystalline pieces. Its distinctive sulphurous aroma adds a unique note to dishes. Available from *herbies.com.au*.

Suet mix Available from the baking or spice section of the supermarket as a flour and suet mixture. Fresh suet (raw beef or mutton fat) is a different product that needs to be ordered in advance from your butcher. To substitute it in recipes, freeze and then grate it into a bowl and rub in an equal weight of plain flour until it comes together to form a texture similar to coarse breadcrumbs.

Sumac A spice with a tangy, lemony taste that is made from the dried berries of a shrub that grows in the Mediterranean and Middle East. Available from specialty food stores, good delis and larger supermarkets.

Tomatoes – heirloom (black russian, ox heart) A wide range of heirloom variety tomatoes with a true tomato taste is now increasingly available in larger supermarkets and greengrocers. Experiment to find a variety you like.

Verjuice Made from under-ripe unfermented grapes. It can be used in dressings, sauces, marinades and any dish that needs a dash of acidity. It can replace sour ingredients such as lemon, lime and vinegar. Available from specialty food stores and delis.

Vincotto – fig A condiment made from cooked grape must and figs. Available from specialty food stores and good delis.

Index

LANTERN

Published by the Penguin Group
Penguin Group (Australia)
250 Camberwell Road, Camberwell, Victoria 3124, Australia
(a division of Pearson Australia Group Pty Ltd)
Penguin Group (USA) Inc.
375 Hudson Street, New York, New York 10014, USA
Penguin Group (Canada)
90 Eglinton Avenue East, Suite 700, Toronto, Canada ON M4P 2Y3
(a division of Pearson Penguin Canada Inc.)
Penguin Books Ltd
80 Strand, London WC2R 0RL, England
Penguin Ireland
25 St Stephen's Green, Dublin 2, Ireland
(a division of Penguin Books Ltd)
Penguin Books India Pvt Ltd
11 Community Centre, Panchsheel Park, New Delhi – 110 017, India
Penguin Group (NZ)
67 Apollo Drive, Rosedale, North Shore 0632, New Zealand
(a division of Pearson New Zealand Ltd)
Penguin Books (South Africa) (Pty) Ltd
24 Sturdee Avenue, Rosebank, Johannesburg 2196, South Africa

Penguin Books Ltd, Registered Offices: 80 Strand, London WC2R 0RL,
England

First published by Penguin Group (Australia), 2010

10 9 8 7 6 5 4 3 2 1

Text copyright © Gary Mehigan and George Calombaris 2010
Photography © Mark Chew and Simon Griffiths 2010
Illustrations © Andrew Joyner 2010

The moral right of the authors has been asserted

Design by Kirby Armstrong © Penguin Group (Australia)
Photography by Mark Chew and Simon Griffiths; styling by Caroline Velik
Illustrations by Andrew Joyner
Cover photography by Mark Chew
Typeset in Chapparal Pro 10.35/14pt by Post Pre-press Group,
Carina Heights, Queensland
Colour reproduction by Splitting Image Colour Studio Pty Ltd, Clayton
Victoria
Printed and bound in China by 1010 Printing International Ltd

National Library of Australia
Cataloguing-in-Publication data:

Mehigan, Gary; Calombaris, George

Your place or mine / Gary Mehigan , George Calombaris
photographers, Mark Chew, Simon Griffiths; illustrator, Andrew Joyner.

9781921382437 (hbk.)

Includes index.
Cookery.

641.6

penguin.com.au/lantern

Thanks

Gary To my wife Mandy – when things get out of focus, I look into those
baby blues and remember why I fell in love – thank you, my darling. To
Jenna, thanks for your hugs and giggles – my world melts around them.

There is no doubt that *MasterChef Australia* has turned my world upside
down. Matt, George and I look at each other once in a while and chuckle.
We are very lucky blokes who share a common bond – we adore food.

George, thank you for being a good friend – you have been a confidante,
professional inspiration (not just to me, but for many), you have a strong
spirit and a good heart and deserve all the happiness life can bring.

To the *MasterChef* team, you are a fabulous bunch and I feel privileged
to be part of it all. I love going to work every day – thank you!

To Justine May, thanks for working tirelessly to stoke the fire and keep
all the wheels turning – it wouldn't be possible without you. I also thank
Michel Roux for his kind words; you have been a culinary idol for so
many years.

To Jason Dixon and Tracy Robertson, thanks again for translating the
recipes into something we can all make and enjoy in our kitchens at home.

George Creating a great cookbook takes a lot of time and commitment.
Without the support of those around me this wouldn't have been possible.
The love I have for my work and my restaurants excites me each day.
I work with a great bunch of people. The support of my business partners,
especially when I'm away filming, gives me peace of mind that our common
interest (to be the best in our field) is achieved every day. Thanks guys!
To the people that represent me and take pride in what they do because
they love it – my front-of-house staff and team of chefs – your passion
resonates to give our customers an exciting dining experience. To my one
hundred and forty staff who work tirelessly at The Press Club, Maha Bar
and Grill, Hellenic Republic and St Katherine's, thank you so much.

Making sure my recipes work in your kitchen is vital, so thanks Justin
Wise for the countless hours spent testing them. Driving my calendar
is Lauren Calleja. She co-ordinates all my madness and makes sure I am
organised (with everything!). Thanks Loz.

To my family – Dad, Mum, Nick and Nicole – your patience and
understanding of my busy life is so appreciated. And to my mate Gary
Mehigan, who has seen my career grow and has supported me throughout.
From being his apprentice to working with him side by side, I am deeply
honoured to have compiled this amazing book together. A big thanks to
my other family of beautiful people that work so hard creating *MasterChef
Australia* and making me look good – you too, Matt!

Last but not least, thanks to the beautiful woman that supports me
every day and never judges me. I love you dearly. Thanks Twika xxx.

From both of us Huge thanks to our publisher, Julie Gibbs – you
light up the room with your enthusiasm, and whenever we see you we find
ourselves smiling long after you're gone – thank you xxx!

Special thanks also to the Penguin team of managing editor Ingrid
Ohlsson, editor Kathleen Gandy, designers Kirby Armstrong and Daniel
New, photographic shoot coordinator Megan Pigott, and production
controller Tracey Jarrett. A huge thanks to journalist Sally Webb, who
turned our thoughts into words so skillfully, and Christine Osmond,
who retested our recipes from the perspective of a busy home cook.
A special thanks to photographers Mark Chew and Simon Griffiths, stylist
Caroline Velik and illustrator Andrew Joyner. Wow! You made it so easy
and made every recipe jump out from the page. This book looks hot!